12·29·70

McCALL'S
Introduction to
FRENCH
COOKING

McCALL'S
Introduction to
FRENCH
COOKING

The McCall Publishing Company

NEW YORK

Library of Congress Catalog Card Number: 73–134480

SBN 8415–0056–8

Printed in the United States of America

Design by Tere LoPrete

Contents

Illustrations follow pages 26, 42, 58, and 74

McCALL'S
Introduction to
FRENCH
COOKING

Introduction

One hundred and fifty years ago a famous French chef living in England complained irascibly that all sorts of inferior people were being granted the title of artist while he himself was denied it: "Even a scraper of catgut in an orchestra calls himself an artist; another, who makes pirouettes and jumps like a kangaroo on the stage, is dignified with the same title. And yet to a man who has under his sole direction those great feasts given by the nobility of England . . . to such a man is denied that title of artist!" The proud chef, Louis Eustache Ude, who had once cooked for Louis XVI himself, would not be so unhappy today. In our time French cooking has come to be recognized as an art indeed. And no wonder. The French seem to look for the hidden flavor locked within a piece of meat in much the same way a sculptor looks for the shape hidden within a block of wood or marble. The French approach the food on their plates with an eye toward the visual, toward the arrangement of shapes and colors. And in the pot, the equivalent of the painter's palette, they are concerned with the blends among foods, the delicate variations and shadings that can be obtained by increasing or decreasing certain ingredients, adding one flavor, subtracting another.

Does this mean that French cooking is more difficult than other styles of cooking? Not at all. There are a wealth of French recipes that are simple and that do not require elaborate equipment or hard-to-get ingredients or even an excessive time investment. They do call for attention on the part of the cook, a willingness to follow instructions: to use butter when the recipe says butter; to use a dry red wine when the recipe so stipulates; to stir the sauces well and beat the eggs with enthusiasm. But beyond that, the combinations of flavors and ingredients in French recipes will almost certainly assure even the most inexperienced cook an impressive result for her efforts. "Make it simple!" warned the greatest French chef of all, Escoffier, to his many disciples. Although he invented in his lifetime over 7,000 recipes and is perhaps the most famous cook of modern times, he never failed to admonish other cooks that simplicity was essential—otherwise the spirit would flag and enthusiasm would depart. The recipes collected here follow the great master's advice and can be mastered by even an inexperienced cook as long as she brings to her efforts the French love of good food.

There are, in fact, two distinctly different types of French cooking. There is grande or haute cuisine, the cooking done by chefs and available in elegant restaurants. And there is provincial cooking. This does not mean unsophisticated—the way in which we use the word provincial—but rather, home cooking; it refers to the kind of food you will eat if you travel in the various French provinces.

Haute cuisine was the creation of men like Francatelli, the chef to Queen Victoria, who insisted that to make a stock that was any good at all one simply had to have forty pounds each of veal and beef, plus many additional pounds of lean ham, carrots, turnips, celery and leeks, and also wild rabbits or hens depending on whether you intended to make a brown or white sauce. It is a very special and professional type of cooking. And in a sense it has been responsible for discouraging many young cooks from attempting French cooking.

But French home cooking is within the reach of all of us. It too is a superior cuisine. In the provinces of France, old recipes have been kept alive over the centuries because they were tried and found to be good. They have been retained and refined. Each area of the country has its own specialties and each has contributed its own best dishes, preserved over the years, to compose what is today the cooking of France.

Why is French cooking—French home cooking—considered so superior to other styles of cooking? What is it about the French? One dramatic difference between the French and the Americans and the French and many other peoples is the attention they pay to eating. Throughout France, in the towns and countryside and even, when possible, in the big cities, the main meal of the day is around noon. The husband comes home from his work, the children from school. And the family gathers together to eat slowly and attentively—a meal well worth their gathering. It is a big meal—a meal composed of one or two courses, as is usual in America, would not seem sufficient to the French. They have eaten sparingly at breakfast—merely some croissants and café au lait, or perhaps some baguettes, the long thin crispy French bread, spread with jam. Now at midday they will sit down to a feast.

The meal always begins with an hors d'oeuvre, a tempting palate teaser that is always served at the table, not beforehand with drinks and apéritifs. Whether simple or elaborate, hot or cold, it is always very flavorful yet very light, designed to tease the palate, not to satiate it. Its name literally means "aside from the main work," and it is a course aside from the main work of dining. It may have required next to no preparation, like a plate of stuffed eggs sprinkled colorfully with paprika, or tangy anchovies laid upon tomato slices, or some marinated mushrooms or zucchini strips. Or it may have required a good deal of work; it can be a homemade pâté, a quiche Lorraine, or a crêpe stuffed with saucy seafood. But whatever it is it must complement what is to follow. If the main course is to be a delicate veal in cream sauce, no French cook would ever serve so strongly flavored an hors d'oeuvre as anchovies and tomatoes; nor would a filling quiche or crêpe be served before a hearty beef bourguignon.

Very often the hors d'oeuvre consists of a variety of tidbits, and it is said to require—as we say weddings require something old, something new, something borrowed, and something blue—something crisp, something salty, something dry, and something smooth: some crisp fresh vegetables, whether new radishes or celery; some salty fish like herrings or anchovies or sardines; some dry and meaty taste, like spicy sausages or ham; and a bland smooth taste, like homemade mayonnaise over eggs or a sauce rémoulade on shrimp. No matter what the social or economic condition of a French diner, he expects his noon meal to begin with an hors d'oeuvre. He expects that dining will be composed of many parts, each planned in relation to the whole.

Some families will then have a fish course. But this is not essential in the way the hors d'oeuvre is. If there is a fish course, the main dish will be meat or poultry. Otherwise the main dish may be fish or meat or poultry.

There are of course thousands of French recipes for main courses. The French eat beef and pork, poultry and many kinds of fish just as we do. But they are more experimental and experienced than we are, and with their great skills at cookery they can add to their list of main course dishes delicious foods that are all too often spurned in America. The American traveling in France will taste and love, and he will wonder why he does not often get such tasty dishes at home as snails, frogs' legs, minnows, eels, brains, tripe, and sweetbreads. Why such foods, disdained here, are so good in France is that they are given the same care there that an expensive steak or bird demands. The best white wine may be lavished on tripe à la mode de Caen, the most tedious care on dipping tiny minnows into a batter of flour and beer and frying them while keeping each one separate from the rest with a quickly moving fork. Nothing edible is too small or too inexpensive for care and the companionship of fine ingredients.

With or after their main course the French eat vegetables. They have special techniques with vegetables that are the essence of simplicity, yet produce remarkable results. To retain the freshness and greenness of vegetables a French woman may boil them in a large quantity of water, then plunge them when barely cooked into an equally large amount of very cold water. This technique is called refreshing and does just that. Refreshed with cold water the quickly cooked vegetables are drained and amazingly keep all their flavor and color until later when they may be reheated in butter just before serving. Another technique the French are fond of is called braising. Vegetables are steamed in a covered saucepan in only a tiny amount of water. This is a good method for preserving the healthful vitamins of vegetables. The water in which the vegetables cook contains all the vitamins and is not discarded but, being slight, is poured over the vegetables when they are served. A third technique is glazing; it is used most often with carrots or onions. They are steamed in a little stock to which sugar has been added to give them a pretty shiny glaze.

Potatoes are considered a vegetable in France and are cooked in a hundred different ways. They are not served as we serve them, merely as an accompaniment to meat. Sometimes, combined with milk or eggs or cheese, they even compose a main dish at supper. The basic and ever-present starch on the Frenchman's table—comparable to our potatoes, the Italians' pasta, and the Orientals' rice—is bread. It is brought to the table with the hors d'oeuvre and it remains on the table throughout the meal. Since the most frequent family dessert in France is cheese and fruit, more bread often appears to accompany them. French bread is delicious in itself and is useful for scraping up whatever last bits of delicious soups or sauces the cook produces. Fortunately French bread is increasingly

available in the United States. Where it is not, the spirited consumer
ought to demand it. There seems little reason for sophisticated Americans
to put up with the soggy mash we call bread.

After the main course and vegetables, the French eat their salad. Salad
comes last because it clears the palate. Seasoned with oil and vinegar
and herbs, it is like a tonic. It perks up the appetite once again for what
is to follow. As with the hors d'oeuvre, salad is essential for the way it
fits into the meal plan. To go from a hearty main dish right to dessert
would fail to give the stomach and palate the moments of clearing and
refreshment that they need and that the cool taste of salad brings.

For dessert, as we have mentioned, the French most often eat cheese
and fruit. Fruit is served with a knife and a fork and on a plate so that one
may truly eat and savor it. Nothing could be more different from the way
we serve fruit. We tend to grab it up from a kitchen bowl and devour it
in a few unthinking gulps. But sit down one day with a juicy pear or
some fresh sweet peaches, peel them, then cut them into bites and
notice—taking time to do it—how exquisite they are.

They are even better with cheese. French cheeses are, of course, superb
and world renowned. Most popular is Camembert, which, when ripe,
should be a light pale yellow with a definite taste and a texture that is
so tender it is almost but not quite runny. Brie is the next most popular.
It too has a soft texture and a definite taste; it too should have the same
soft almost runny consistency.

Other popular French cheeses are Roquefort, which is salty and tangy;
Cantal, France's only cheddarlike cheese, semihard and smooth; and
Reblochon, a soft cream-colored cheese whose texture is similar to Camembert but which does not get runny. But these are only tiny jewels in the
crown that is composed of French cheeses.

There are dozens and dozens of cheeses, from hard to soft. Goat cheese
in particular is delicious, as are the little creamy cheeses like Boursin
Triple-crème and Belletoile Triple-crème, which are so rich they are
frequently eaten all by themselves, doused with powdered sugar to
sweeten them, as a true dessert.

All French cheeses should be served at room temperature. They must
be removed from the refrigerator one to three hours before serving.
Again, the cheese should be picked to complement the fruit. Roquefort,
with its strong flavor, goes well with pears, which are mild. Cantal goes
well with tart apples or green grapes. But tasting will soon determine
one's own favorite pairs.

On Sundays or holidays in France there may be a cooked dessert in place of the fruit and cheese. It may be a mousse or pots de crème à la vanille or little pastries from the best local pâtisserie. Cooked desserts are for special meals, but in France, as here, housewives love to make them and every woman has a repertoire of her own favorites.

Now, and only now, comes coffee. Although the French drink coffee with their breakfast rolls, they disdain it as part of a meal. It is the end and not the accompaniment to dining.

Wine, of course, has been drunk throughout the meal. It is beyond the scope of this introduction to acquaint the reader with all the mystique and lore of French wines. But it is important to note that a French meal without French wine is, as the old song goes, like a man without a woman or a boat without a sail. Wine is considered as necessary to the meal as the bread or even the meat itself. There are a few easy rules to follow about wine: A cool dry white wine is best for almost all hors d'oeuvres and for all fish; a dry red wine at room temperature is best for meats and cheeses; a slightly sweeter and perhaps sparkling wine may be served with pies and pastries and desserts. Dry white wines are always served before red wines, which are heavier. If two white wines or two red wines are to be served, the lighter and drier must always come before the heavier one; the less important before the most prestigious; and almost always, the younger before the elder unless for some reason the vintage year of the younger is a particularly exciting one.

The French do not drink cocktails. Strong alcohol detracts from the pleasures of the palate by dulling the taste buds. Wine does not do this. The French do take a wine-based apéritif before a meal and more and more often one finds in France a premeal drinking time that is comparable to our cocktail hour. It is a family affair, however. Even the children are invited, and they are given wine diluted with water.

No introduction to French cooking would be complete without mentioning the importance of herbs. However, one does not need to have a huge spice rack to house the herbs necessary for even the most intricate French cooking. The French do not use a lot of herbs. There are only twelve very commonly encountered herbs, and of these one can manage quite adequately with only five or six.

The twelve used most often are chives, bay leaves, rosemary, sage, savory, tarragon, thyme, parsley, basil, chervil, fennel, and marjoram. Chives are related to onions and go well in bland dishes and salads. Bay leaves are strong and fragrant and can flavor stronger dishes, soups and stews, and vegetable concoctions. Rosemary is sweet and is used with meats. Sage is slightly bitter and very perfumed. Savory has a gentle flavor and goes well on delicate vegetables. Tarragon is licoricelike and tastes best on chicken and fish. Thyme is fragrant and has a strong taste, again best for soups and stews. Parsley, with its slightly peppery taste, is good on almost anything, as is basil, which is related to mint. Chervil is similar to parsley; fennel is licoricelike; marjoram mintlike.

Of these, an American housewife attempting to learn French cooking would do well to stock parsley, thyme, bay leaf, and tarragon in their bottled forms, and to obtain fresh parsley and chervil when possible. When fresh parsley, chives, tarragon, and chervil are mixed together, they are called fines herbes. And when parsley, thyme, and bay leaves are tied together, the bundle is called an herb bouquet, or bouquet garni.

Fresh herbs are better than dried ones because they are much more flavorful. Interestingly, they are not at all difficult to grow. They can be placed in a tiny herb garden outside the kitchen door. Or, if you do not have space, they can easily be grown in pots, either outdoors on terraces or indoors by sunny windows. They are most delicious when fresh but can be dried and stored for later use. The best way to dry them is to pick them early in the morning and dry them in the sun for a few hours. Then they should be tied in bunches and hung upside down or else spread on a piece of door or window screen that is elevated above the floor so that air can circulate above and below them.

The story of how French cooking achieved its worldwide eminence is as interesting as the dishes and ingredients themselves. In the Middle Ages the French cooked very much the way the rest of the world did. But in 1533, when Italy's Catherine de Médicis married Henry, France's Duke of Orleans, more than a marriage of two individuals occurred. The Italian princess brought with her to France as part of her dowry her renowned Italian chefs. The Duke, of course, had some distinguished chefs of his own. Both groups were competing for royal favor, and somehow there occurred a marriage of culinary styles between the two. A new cuisine began to develop in France, one combining all the best techniques of the time.

Its prestige spread to England when Charles II became king of England in 1661. He had been living in exile in France, afraid to return to his own country of "king-killers." But when he was finally enthroned, he brought with him French chefs and the French style of eating, more elegant, more refined than that of England. The English upper classes began to recognize that their own ways of preparing food were oversimple and dull, and they began hiring French chefs. But the final impetus was provided by the French Revolution.

The Bourbon kings were all gourmets. Louis XIII had a do-it-yourself approach to cooking that would have made him quite at home at America's backyard barbecues. He both killed and prepared his own game. Louis XIV was lazier or perhaps just a better administrator; he chose geniuses to cook for him, including the great Béchamel, for whom one of France's greatest sauces is named. Under Louis XIV, chefs achieved a place of enormous prominence. They wrote books, made pronouncements, and were even known to commit suicide when things went badly at their meals. Louis XV loved to drink champagne and eat cold lark pâtés, and it was said that eating was the only serious occupation of his life. This concern with appetite and self-indulgence ran in the Bourbon family. Even the in-laws shared it, as witnessed by Marie Antoinette's famous "let-them-eat-cake" remark. But when the French decided that the Bourbons were after all just another part of the family of man, they also seem to have decided that all men should share in the family trait. When the French killed Louis XVI and Marie Antoinette, they indirectly spread the best French cuisine throughout all France and the rest of the world.

For the Revolution not only killed the king and queen and a lot of nobles but it also created mass unemployment among chefs. Because of their close association with the nobility, chefs were in danger. Some went into hiding, others into exile. But as soon as the initial republican violence had worn off, a few of them emerged with a fantastic moneymaking idea. The French nobles were gone or had been guillotined. All the more reason to gird up the people of France to their new duty as keepers of the culture of France. Rather than destroying the chefs of the nobility, the chefs argued that the people should appropriate them as they had appropriated the tapestries and paintings and furniture of the nobles' homes. This was the idea that occurred to the chefs, and it was the start of restaurants as we now know them.

There had been a few places serving food before the Revolution, but they were primarily inns whose idea of food was merely survival fare, food as a means of keeping the traveler alive as he passed from one place to another. But when the chefs of the nobility began opening places to dine, and it was reported about that the very men who had catered to the refined palates of the courtiers were now selling food to any republican with the price of his meal, restaurants began to flourish.

With them flourished the eminence of French cooking and it has continued to do so for two centuries. Invariably, once people are exposed to the tastes of fine French dishes, all other food seems pale by comparison. And invariably, learning how to cook in the French style brings a hostess into eminence too.

Hors d'Oeuvres

It is common in France to begin lunch or dinner with an hors d'oeuvre or first course. As a first course dish, the hors d'oeuvre is calculated to whet the appetite for the food that is to come, and usually it is not served in large portions. A beginning course like this also has the advantage of making the expensive meat course go further. In France, an hors d'oeuvre selection (hors d'oeuvres variés) is also served as the main course of a light lunch or supper, particularly in summer. Preceded by a filling soup like Onion au Gratin, an assorted hors d'oeuvre platter, or a salad—the "composed" salads of cooked vegetables or seafood that the French are so fond of—is a satisfying meal.

Often, for a family-style meal, a sampling of several kinds of appetizers —cold vegetables in vinaigrette sauce, sliced meats, sausages from the charcuterie (a combination butcher shop and delicatessen), homemade pâtés—is served with crusty French bread and chilled white wine. Attractively arranged and decorated with bright green chopped parsley, these selections of hors d'oeuvres often include leftovers from previous meals. It is a thrifty and agreeable practice in French households to use up yesterday's green beans, an extra hard-boiled egg, a few shrimp, or the end of a roast in this way. Small canapé-type hors d'oeuvres, so often served in America, are almost unknown in the average French home.

The first course for company meals, holidays and Sundays, and festive dinners is more elaborate than the everyday hors d'oeuvre selection. Usually, the servings are more substantial—for instance, a first course portion of Snails in Garlic Butter would be six to eight snails, whereas three to four would suffice for an hors d'oeuvre serving. The company dinner is the time to serve an elaborate Pâté en Croûte; while a slice of the simpler Terrine of Country Pâté with bread and a few radishes with butter would be a suitable family-type hors d'oeuvre. The delicious quiches— open tarts with custard-type fillings, flavored with cheese and bacon or crab meat—are substantial first courses and should be followed by a roast, steak, or chops. A cold Quiche Lorraine is also good picnic food.

Very elegant first courses include crêpes rolled around crab meat or curried chicken and an entire Camembert wrapped in a pastry crust. Dishes like these at a dinner show that the cook not only is offering her guests fine food but that she also enjoys preparing it, a characteristic of the French homemaker.

Many of the recipes in this chapter can also be served as a main course either for lunch or dinner. Judge the amount to serve—whether as a beginning or main course—by the rest of the menu.

COLD VEGETABLES AND COMBINATION SALADS
Légumes Froids et Salades Composées

Artichokes with Tarragon Butter
ARTICHAUTS AU BEURRE D'ESTRAGON

¼ cup olive or salad oil
6 slices lemon
2 bay leaves
1 clove garlic, split
1 teaspoon salt
⅛ teaspoon pepper
4 large artichokes
   (about 3 pounds)

Tarragon Butter
½ cup melted butter
2 tablespoons olive oil
2 tablespoons lemon juice
1 tablespoon dried tarragon
   leaves

1. In large kettle, combine 3 quarts water with ¼ cup olive oil, the lemon slices, bay leaves, garlic, salt, and pepper; bring to boiling.
2. Meanwhile, trim stalk from base of each artichoke; cut off 1 inch from tops. Remove discolored leaves; snip off spike ends of leaves.
3. Wash the artichokes in cold water; drain.
4. Add to boiling mixture. Reduce heat; simmer, covered, 40 to 45 min-

utes, or until artichoke bases feel soft. Drain artichokes well. Refrigerate until well chilled—several hours.

5. Meanwhile, make Tarragon Butter: In a small bowl, mix butter, olive oil, lemon juice, and tarragon until well combined.

6. To serve: Place a chilled artichoke and a small cup of sauce on each individual plate.

Makes 4 servings.

Artichoke-Heart Salad

SALADE DE FONDS D'ARTICHAUTS

1 package (9 ounces) frozen
   artichoke hearts
¼ cup cider vinegar
¼ cup salad or olive oil
2 tablespoons thinly sliced
   green onion
1½ teaspoons sugar

⅛ teaspoon dry mustard
⅛ teaspoon salt
Dash pepper
1 or 2 heads Bibb lettuce,
   washed and crisped
8 cherry tomatoes

1. Cook frozen artichoke hearts in slightly salted water, as package label directs. Drain. Place in pie plate.

2. In jar with tight-fitting lid, combine vinegar, oil, onion, sugar, mustard, salt, and pepper. Shake well to combine.

3. Pour dressing over artichokes. Refrigerate, covered and stirring once or twice, until well chilled—at least 2 hours.

4. Arrange lettuce in salad bowl. Top with artichokes and tomatoes.

5. Just before serving, drizzle with remaining dressing from artichokes.

Makes 2 servings.

Marinated Asparagus

ASPERGES VINAIGRETTE

2 packages (10-ounce size)
   frozen asparagus spears

⅓ cup bottled oil-and-vinegar
   dressing

1. Cook asparagus as package label directs. Drain well. Place in shallow dish.

2. Pour dressing over asparagus. Refrigerate, covered, until well chilled—at least 2 hours.

Makes 6 servings.

Celeriac in Rémoulade Dressing

CÉLERI-RAVE AU SAUCE RÉMOULADE

5 medium celeriac, pared (2¼ pounds)	1 tablespoon finely chopped parsley
2 cups mayonnaise, or cooked salad dressing	½ teaspoon dried tarragon leaves
2 hard-cooked eggs, finely chopped	½ teaspoon dried chervil leaves
½ cup chopped sour pickles	1 medium tomato
2 tablespoons pickle juice	
2 tablespoons finely chopped capers	Watercress
1 tablespoon tarragon vinegar	Hard-cooked egg wedges
	Capers

1. In boiling salted water to cover, cook celeriac, covered, 5 minutes. Drain; let cool.

2. In medium bowl, combine mayonnaise, chopped eggs, pickles, pickle juice, chopped capers, vinegar, parsley, tarragon, and chervil; mix well.

3. Coarsely grate celeriac, and stir into mayonnaise mixture. Slice tomato, and discard seeds. Chop tomato coarsely. Add to celeriac mixture; mix just until blended.

4. Refrigerate, covered, until well chilled—several hours, or overnight.

5. To serve: Garnish with watercress, egg wedges, and capers. Makes 12 servings.

Marinated Mushrooms

CHAMPIGNONS MAÎTRE D'HÔTEL

8 fresh mushrooms	½ teaspoon salt
¼ cup herb-garlic salad dressing	⅛ teaspoon pepper
½ cup butter or margarine	3 tablespoons finely chopped parsley
2 tablespoons lemon juice	

1. Wash mushrooms; dry with paper towels. Remove stems.

2. Toss mushroom caps with dressing. Refrigerate until needed.

3. In small bowl, beat butter until smooth. Beat in lemon juice, salt, pepper, and parsley until blended. Put butter mixture in pastry bag with star tip.

4. Drain mushroom caps. Fill with butter mixture, swirling it attractively. Refrigerate mushrooms until serving time.

Makes 4 or 8 servings.

Mediterranean Combination Salad

SALADE NIÇOISE

Dressing
½ cup olive oil
¼ cup salad oil
¼ cup red-wine vinegar
1 teaspoon sugar
¾ teaspoon salt
¼ teaspoon cracked pepper

Salad
1 pound fresh green beans,
   trimmed and washed; or
   2 packages (9-ounce size)
   frozen whole green beans

1 medium red onion, thinly sliced
2 medium tomatoes, cut in
   wedges
½ cup pitted ripe olives
1 can (2 ounces) anchovy fillets
2 cans (7-ounce size) solid-pack
   tuna, drained and broken
   into chunks
2 hard-cooked eggs, sliced

1. Make Dressing: In jar with tight-fitting lid, combine oils, vinegar, sugar, salt, and pepper; shake vigorously until well combined.

2. Cook whole fresh beans in small amount of boiling salted water, covered, 17 to 20 minutes, or until tender. Cook frozen beans, as package label directs, 5 minutes, or just until tender. Drain well; turn into shallow dish. Add ½ cup dressing; toss until beans are well coated.

3. Refrigerate beans, covered. Also refrigerate remaining dressing and the salad ingredients until well chilled—at least 2 hours.

4. To serve: Turn green beans into salad bowl. Add all but a few onion slices, tomato wedges, olives, and anchovy fillets; toss gently. Then add tuna chunks, egg slices; toss again.

5. Garnish with reserved onion, tomato, olives, and anchovy. Drizzle remaining dressing over all.

Makes 6 servings.

Snails in Garlic Butter

ESCARGOTS À LA BOURGUIGNONNE

1 can snails with shells
   (7½-ounce can, 1½ dozen
   shells)
½ cup soft butter or margarine
2 or 3 cloves garlic, crushed
1 shallot, finely chopped

1½ tablespoons finely chopped
   parsley
1 tablespoon lemon juice
¾ teaspoon salt
¾ teaspoon dried chervil leaves

1. Prepare several hours before serving. Wash snail shells, and drain well on paper towels. Drain snails thoroughly; set aside.

2. In medium bowl, combine butter with remaining ingredients; mix well.

3. Place a little butter mixture—a generous ¼ teaspoon—in each shell. Push a drained snail into each shell; cover with more butter mixture.

4. Arrange filled shells carefully, open ends up, in a flat baking dish or special escargot (snail) dishes. Cover, and refrigerate.

5. To serve: Preheat oven to 400°F. Bake snails in shells, uncovered, 8 to 10 minutes, or until butter mixture is very bubbly. Serve immediately.

Makes 4 first-course or 6 to 8 hors-d'oeuvre servings.

Camembert in Pastry Crust

CAMEMBERT EN CROÛTE

½ cup sifted all-purpose flour	¼ cup butter or regular
⅛ teaspoon salt	margarine
2 ounces cream cheese	
(¼ cup)	1 Camembert cheese (see Note)
	1 egg yolk
	2 teaspoons water

1. Make pastry day before: Sift flour with salt into medium bowl.

2. With pastry blender, cut in cream cheese and butter until mixture resembles coarse crumbs.

3. Shape pastry into a ball; flatten slightly. Wrap in plastic film or bag. Refrigerate overnight.

4. Start making Camembert en Croûte about 3 hours before serving. On lightly floured pastry cloth or board, roll out pastry to ⅛-inch (not less) thickness.

5. With pastry wheel or knife, cut out a 7-inch circle; place on cookie sheet. Set Camembert cheese in center of circle. Bring pastry up around side and ½ inch over top of cheese, taking care not to stretch or tear pastry and pressing pastry smooth.

6. Roll out trimmings. With a pastry wheel, cut out a circle to fit top of cheese exactly.

7. In small bowl, with a fork, beat egg yolk and 2 teaspoons water. Brush some of egg mixture on pastry rim around top edge of cheese. Place pastry circle on top.

8. With pastry wheel, cut 2 strips, 5 inches long and ½ inch wide, and

3 leaves from remaining pastry. Roll up each strip, to resemble a rosebud. Place, with leaves, in center of pastry. Brush top and decoration lightly with rest of egg mixture.

9. Refrigerate at least 1 hour before baking.

10. Preheat oven to 425°F.

11. Bake 20 minutes, or until pastry is golden brown. Let cool on cookie sheet on wire rack at room temperature 30 minutes.

12. Remove to serving board or plate. Cut in wedges, and serve on small plates.

Makes 6 servings.

Note: Buy a 7- or 8-ounce Camembert cheese, 4 inches in diameter and 1 inch high.

Crêpes Filled with Curried Chicken
CRÊPES DE POULET À L'INDIENNE

Chicken Filling
5 tablespoons butter or margarine
¼ cup all-purpose flour
Salt
1½ cups milk
1 teaspoon chopped shallot or green onion
2 cups cooked chicken or turkey in ¼-inch cubes
½ cup dry white wine
1 teaspoon curry powder
¼ teaspoon Worcestershire sauce
⅛ teaspoon pepper
Dash cayenne

Crêpes
1 cup milk
¾ cup unsifted all-purpose flour
¼ teaspoon salt
2 eggs

Salad oil

Topping
1 egg yolk
⅛ teaspoon salt
4 tablespoons butter or margarine, melted
2 teaspoons lemon juice
¼ cup heavy cream, whipped

Grated Parmesan cheese

1. Make Chicken Filling: To make white sauce, melt 4 tablespoons butter in medium saucepan; remove from heat. Stir in ¼ cup flour and ½ teaspoon salt until smooth. Gradually stir in milk; bring to boiling, stirring constantly. Reduce heat and simmer 5 minutes. Remove from heat, and set aside.

2. In 1 tablespoon hot butter in medium skillet, sauté shallot 1 minute. Add chicken; sauté 2 minutes longer. Add wine, curry, ¼ teaspoon salt,

the Worcestershire, pepper, and cayenne; cook over medium heat, stirring 3 minutes. Stir in 1 cup of the white sauce just until blended. Refrigerate while making crêpes. Set aside remaining white sauce for topping.

3. Make Crêpes: In medium bowl, with rotary beater, beat milk with flour and salt until smooth. Add eggs; beat until well combined.

4. Slowly heat a 5½-inch skillet until a little water sizzles when dropped on it. Brush pan lightly with salad oil. Pour about 1½ tablespoons batter into skillet, tilting pan so batter covers bottom.

5. Cook until nicely browned on underside. Loosen edge; turn; cook until browned on other side. Remove from pan; cool on wire rack. Then stack on waxed paper. Repeat with rest of batter, to make 18 crêpes. Lightly brush pan with oil before cooking each one.

6. Preheat oven to 350°F. Remove filling from refrigerator. Spoon 1 rounded tablespoon onto each crêpe; fold two opposite sides over filling. Arrange in shallow baking dish, seam side up; cover with foil. Bake 20 to 25 minutes, or until heated through.

7. Meanwhile, make Topping: In small bowl, with rotary beater, beat egg yolk with salt until foamy. Gradually beat in 2 tablespoons melted butter. Mix remaining butter with lemon juice; gradually beat into egg-yolk mixture. With wire whisk or rubber scraper, fold in remaining white sauce just until combined. Fold in whipped cream.

8. Uncover hot crêpes. Spoon topping over them; sprinkle lightly with grated Parmesan cheese. Broil, 4 to 6 inches from heat, until nicely browned. If desired, carefully transfer to chafing dish.

Makes 8 servings.

To prepare ahead of time: Make and fill crêpes as directed. Cover with foil, and refrigerate. Make topping, but do not add whipped cream. Refrigerate. To serve: Bake crêpes as directed. Fold the whipped cream into topping; spoon over the crêpes. Sprinkle with cheese; broil as directed.

Cheese and Bacon Quiche

QUICHE LORRAINE

9-inch unbaked pie shell	1½ cups light cream
½ pound sliced bacon	¾ teaspoon salt
1½ cups grated natural Swiss	Dash nutmeg
cheese (6 ounces)	Dash cayenne
3 eggs	Dash pepper

1. Prepare pie shell. Refrigerate until ready to use. Preheat the oven to 375°F.

2. Fry bacon until crisp; drain on paper towels. Crumble bacon into bits, and sprinkle over bottom of prepared pie shell. Then sprinkle with grated Swiss cheese.

3. In medium bowl, with rotary beater, beat eggs with light cream, salt, nutmeg, cayenne, and pepper until well combined but not frothy. Pour into pie shell.

4. Bake 35 to 40 minutes, or until the top is golden and the center seems firm when gently shaken. Let Quiche Lorraine cool on a wire rack for 10 minutes before serving.

Makes 6 servings, or 12 hors d'oeuvre servings.

Crab Meat Quiche

QUICHE AUX FRUITS DE MER

9-inch unbaked pie shell	4 eggs
Raw rice	1½ cups light cream
1 can (7¾ ounces) king-crab meat, drained	2 or 3 tablespoons dry sherry
¼ cup chopped green onion	1 teaspoon salt
2 tablespoons chopped parsley	Dash cayenne
½ cup grated Gruyère cheese	Dash pepper

1. Preheat oven to 425°F.

2. Prepare pie shell. Carefully line shell with aluminum foil; fill with raw rice. Bake 15 minutes, or until pastry edges are slightly brown.

3. Remove from oven; remove foil and rice. Bake shell 2 minutes longer. Remove to wire rack. Reduce oven temperature to 350°F.

4. Drain crab meat; break into pieces, discarding any cartilage. Combine in medium bowl with onion and parsley; toss to mix well. Spoon into pie shell, spreading evenly. Sprinkle with cheese.

5. In same bowl, beat eggs with cream, sherry, salt, cayenne, and pepper.

6. Place pie shell on rack in oven; pour egg mixture over cheese in pie shell.

7. Bake 35 to 40 minutes, or just until custard seems set when quiche is gently shaken.

8. Cool on wire rack for 10 minutes. Cut into wedges to serve.

Makes 6 to 8 servings.

Chicken-Liver Pâté

PÂTÉ DE FOIE DE VOLAILLE

Pâté keeps very well under refrigeration. It is sliced for hors d'oeuvres variés and served with French bread and cornichons, small sour pickles, as a substantial first course. Pâtés make perfect picnic food, and with wine, bread, and a bowl of fresh fruit, they make a lovely light meal. Wines to drink with pâtés are the rosés, and young reds such as Beaujolais.

½ cup sweet butter	1½ tablespoons cognac
1 large onion, sliced (1 cup)	½ teaspoon salt
1¼ pounds chicken livers	Dash pepper
1 hard-cooked egg	Chopped green onion

1. In 2 tablespoons hot butter in skillet, sauté sliced onion until tender —about 10 minutes. Remove from skillet.

2. Heat remaining butter in same skillet. Add chicken livers, and sauté over medium heat 3 to 5 minutes, or until golden brown. Liver should be pink inside.

3. Put half the sautéed onion, chicken livers, egg, and cognac in blender; blend at low speed just until smooth. Turn into bowl. Repeat with rest of onion, livers, egg, and cognac. Stir in salt and pepper. Turn into crock or small bowl.

4. Refrigerate, covered, until well chilled—overnight. Garnish with green onion.

Makes 3 cups.

Cold Veal and Ham Pie

PÂTÉ DE VEAU ET JAMBON

1½ pound veal cutlet, ¼ inch thick	¼ teaspoon dried thyme leaves
	Dash pepper
1 pound fully cooked ham slice, ½ inch thick	1½ packages (9.5 ounce size) piecrust mix
2 tablespoons finely chopped onion	1 can (4½ ounces) deviled ham
2 tablespoons finely chopped parsley	4 hard-cooked eggs, shelled
½ teaspoon salt	1 egg, slightly beaten
¼ teaspoon dried marjoram leaves	1 envelope unflavored gelatine
	1 cup chicken broth

1. Wipe veal with damp paper towels. Cut into 12 pieces as even in size as possible; pound each with mallet. Trim excess fat from ham. Cut ham into strips 2 inches by ¾ inch.

2. In small bowl, combine onion, parsley, salt, marjoram, thyme, and pepper; blend well.

3. Preheat oven to 350°F.

4. Prepare piecrust mix as package label directs. Shape into a ball; remove one-third pastry, and set aside.

5. On lightly floured surface, roll out larger portion of pastry into a 12-inch circle. Set aside trimmings. Use to line a 9-inch deep, fluted pie plate, letting pastry stand up around edge.

6. Roll out remaining pastry into an 11-inch circle. Set aside trimmings. Then roll out all trimmings, and cut into diamond-shape pieces, about 1 inch wide and 1¼ inches long, to decorate top of pie.

7. Spread deviled ham over pastry in pie plate. Arrange half of veal in pie plate; sprinkle with half of herb mixture; then add half of ham strips. Arrange whole hard-cooked eggs in center, spoke fashion. Repeat layering, mounding in center over eggs and using rest of veal, herb mixture, and ham.

8. Adjust 11-inch pastry circle over filling. Fold edge of bottom crust over top crust; press the edges together, to seal well; crimp decoratively. With tip of sharp paring knife, cut a 1½-inch round whole in center for steam vent.

9. Arrange diamond-shape pastry pieces on top. Brush with beaten egg.

10. Bake 1½ hours.

11. Meanwhile, sprinkle gelatine over chicken broth in small saucepan; let stand to soften. Heat, stirring, until gelatine is dissolved. Let stand at room temperature.

12. Let pie cool on wire rack 30 minutes. Then slowly pour broth mixture, through a small funnel, into center of pie. Let cool 2 hours longer; then refrigerate, loosely covered, overnight.

Makes 8 to 10 servings.

Note: If traveling to picnic, remove pie from refrigerator just before leaving, and carry in cooler or insulated bag. Remember to take a pie server.

Pâté Baked in a Crust

PÂTÉ EN CROÛTE

Pastry
4 cups unsifted all-purpose
  flour
1 teaspoon salt
⅔ cup butter or margarine
⅔ cup water
2 eggs

Filling
1 pound lean veal round,
  ¼-inch thick, all in ¼-inch
  strips
½ cup chopped shallots
⅔ cup brandy
2 tablespoons butter or
  margarine
1 pound ground veal
¼ pound pork fat, finely chopped
1½ teaspoons salt

1 teaspoon dried thyme leaves
1 can (⅞ ounce) truffles,
  chopped
1 pound ground pork
2 eggs
⅛ teaspoon allspice
⅛ teaspoon pepper
½ pound cooked ham, cut in
  ¼-inch strips
3 bay leaves

1 egg yolk
1 teaspoon water

1 envelope unflavored gelatine
2 cans (10½-ounce size)
  condensed beef consommé,
  undiluted

1. Make Pastry: In large bowl, combine flour and 1 teaspoon salt. With pastry blender, cut in ⅔ cup butter until mixture resembles coarse crumbs.

2. In 2-cup measure, measure ⅔ cup water. Add 2 eggs; beat with fork until well blended. Add to flour mixture all at once; with fork, stir until combined. With hands, knead several times in bowl. Wrap in waxed paper. Refrigerate pastry for several hours.

3. Meanwhile, make Filling: In small bowl, combine veal strips, 1 tablespoon shallots, and 2 tablespoons brandy; mix well. Refrigerate, covered.

4. In hot butter in small skillet, sauté remaining shallots just until tender—about 3 minutes. Add remaining brandy; cook over medium heat about 5 minutes, or until mixture is reduced to ½ cup.

5. In medium bowl, combine ground veal, pork fat, the ½ cup shallot-brandy mixture, 1½ teaspoons salt, and the thyme; mix well. Measure 1 cup mixture into small bowl; add truffles. Set aside. To remaining mixture, add ground pork, 2 eggs, the allspice, and pepper; mix well. Set aside.

6. To prepare mold: Line sides and bottom of 9-by-5-by-3-inch pan with double thickness of heavy duty foil, allowing 1-inch overhang.

7. On lightly floured surface, roll out two-thirds of pastry into a 12-by-15-inch rectangle. Fit into prepared pan so it lines pan completely and is smooth but not stretched. Trim edge, leaving a ½-inch overhang.

8. Set aside 1 cup ground veal-and-pork mixture. Turn remaining into pastry-lined pan, and pat to make a 1-inch-thick layer over bottom and up each side (not ends).

9. Now line sides and bottom with three-quarters of the veal strips, then with three-quarters of the ham strips. Fill center with the reserved veal-truffle mixture. Top with remaining ham strips, then remaining veal strips. Pour any remaining brandy mixture from veal strips over all. Last, add reserved veal-and-pork mixture, patting it into an even layer. Top with bay leaves.

10. Preheat over to 350°F.

11. For top crust, roll out remaining pastry to a 12-by-8-inch rectangle. Beat egg yolk with 1 teaspoon water; brush some around pastry in pan. Add top crust; pinch pastry together at edges to seal; trim off excess.

12. Roll out pastry trimmings. Cut into enough ½-inch-wide fluted strips to edge top. Cut out 5 or 6 leaves with cookie cutter, or ovals with pastry wheel. Cut 3 strips, 5 or 6 inches long and ½ inch wide, and roll up to resemble roses. Brush top crust with egg mixture. Press strips, roses, and leaves in place. With sharp knife, cut 2 holes, ½ inch in diameter, in top crust, for steam vents. Brush decorations with egg mixture. Insert meat thermometer through a steam vent into center of meat.

13. Place foil on rack below to catch drippings. Bake about 2½ hours, or until thermometer registers 180°F. If decoration becomes too brown, cover with small pieces of foil. Remove pâté to wire rack.

14. Sprinkle gelatine over 1 can beef consommé in small saucepan to soften. Place over low heat, stirring constantly, until gelatine is dissolved. Remove from heat; add remaining consommé.

15. With baster, through steam vents, add some consommé mixture to pâté. Keep adding more every 10 or 15 minutes as pâté cools at room temperature—about an hour. Then refrigerate pâté, adding consommé mixture at intervals until all is used. Refrigerate overnight.

16. To serve: With sharp knife, loosen pastry and foil around sides and ends. Then carefully lift out pâté, and peel off foil. Arrange pâté on serving platter. Garnish with watercress, if desired.

Makes 12 servings.

Terrine of Country Pâté

TERRINE DE VEAU AVEC FOIE

1 pound calf's liver	2 tablespoons brandy
¾ pound ground pork fat	2 teaspoons salt
¼ pound ground veal	¾ teaspoon pepper
3 tablespoons butter or	¼ teaspoon allspice
margarine	¼ teaspoon mace
¾ cup chopped onion	6 slices bacon
5 tablespoons flour	1 can (3 ounces) whole
1⅓ cups milk	mushrooms, drained
3 eggs	

1. Rinse liver; pat dry with paper towels. Cut into small pieces. Put through food grinder twice, using finest blade. Or put liver, one-third at a time, in electric blender, and blend at high speed until smooth. Turn into large bowl; stir in pork fat and veal.

2. Preheat oven to 350°F. Grease a 5- or 6-cup casserole.

3. In hot butter in medium saucepan, sauté onion until tender—about 5 minutes. Stir in flour until well combined. Gradually stir in milk; bring to boiling, stirring constantly. Reduce heat, and simmer 1 minute.

4. Add to liver mixture, along with eggs, brandy, salt, pepper, allspice, and mace; stir until well blended. Turn into prepared casserole.

5. Place in roasting pan; pour hot water to 2-inch level around casserole.

6. Bake, uncovered, 1 hour and 45 minutes. Let cool at least 1 hour before serving.

7. Just before serving, in large skillet, fry bacon, until crisp. Drain on paper towels. Pour off all but 2 tablespoons drippings.

8. In hot bacon drippings, sauté mushrooms until golden. Arrange with bacon over pâté. Serve warm, with bread and sweet butter and pickled beets, if desired.

Makes 30 buffet servings.

Note: If pâté is made ahead of time, garnish just before serving.

Soups

Soups are made of the best and freshest possible ingredients in France. Flavorful vegetables, plump chickens, and cuts of beef go into the hearty, meal-in-themselves soups like Pot-au-feu. The seafood for Bouillabaisse, the Mediterranean combination of stew and soup, is as fresh as can be bought; for the best flavor the lobsters and shellfish should be alive and the fish fillets must be firm and sweet. As much care and preparation goes into making soup as goes into a richly sauced dish or an elaborate dessert, for the French take their soups seriously.

Hearty soups, filled with meats and vegetables, such as the cabbage and onion soups of the working man, are considered suitable for the main dish of supper. The soup is always accompanied by bread. A glass of wine, a green salad, cheese, and fruit complete the typical evening menu. Lighter soups, cream soups and consommés, are also served for supper, followed by an omelet, soufflé, or a vegetable dish. In warm weather, a chilled soup and an omelet with bread, salad, and fresh fruit make a satisfying supper, or in the American tradition of eating, a simple luncheon. The chilled vegetable soups are also suitable for the first course of an American formal dinner; in France, only consommés or clear broths are served at dinners.

The heartier soups are served in cold weather; in the warm months lighter ones that depend on spring or summer vegetables or fresh herbs are popular. Spicy, regional soups and the fish stews like Bouillabaisse are served at noon rather than at night so that they may be more easily digested.

Coq au Vin

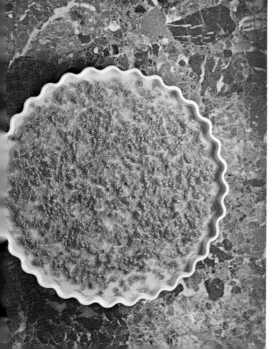

Crème Brûlée

Petits Pois

Raspberries Sabayon

Asparagus with Hollandaise Sauce

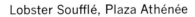
Lobster Soufflé, Plaza Athénée

Jellied Madrilène

CONSOMMÉ MADRILÈNE

1 envelope unflavored gelatine
¼ cup water
2 cans (13-ounce size)
  consommé madrilène

3 tablespoons Madeira
Lemon wedges

1. Sprinkle gelatine over ¼ cup water in small saucepan to soften. Stir in ¼ cup madrilène. Heat, stirring constantly, just until gelatine is dissolved.

2. In medium bowl, stir it into remaining madrilène, along with Madeira. Pour into 13-by-9-by-2-inch pan.

3. Refrigerate until firm—at least 2 hours.

4. To serve: Cut jellied madrilène into ½-inch cubes. Spoon into individual chilled bouillon cups. Garnish with lemon wedges.

Makes 6 servings.

Chilled Leek and Potato Soup

VICHYSSOISE

This is an American adaptation of a French leek and potato soup, Potage Parmentier; it has become an international favorite. Vichyssoise is usually served in the summer and Potage Parmentier in the winter. To make Potage Parmentier, follow the recipe below, substituting milk for the cup of heavy cream. Add all the milk after the vegetable mixture has been strained, then heat slowly, and serve hot.

1½ cups chopped, pared raw
  potato
1½ cups chopped leek (white
  part only)
1 can (10½ ounces) condensed
  chicken broth

1 cup milk
1 cup heavy cream
½ teaspoon salt
Dash pepper
2 tablespoons chopped chives

1. In large saucepan, combine potato, leek, undiluted chicken broth, and 1 soup can water. Bring to boiling; reduce heat; simmer, covered, 25 minutes. Vegetables should be very soft.

2. Strain mixture through a sieve, pressing vegetables through. Or blend in an electric blender 1 to 2 minutes, or until smooth.

3. Turn into large bowl. Refrigerate, covered, until it is chilled—about 3 hours.

4. Stir in milk, cream, salt, and pepper until blended. Refrigerate, covered, 2 hours, or until very well chilled.

5. Serve in a large bowl or in bouillon cups, topped with the chopped chives.

Makes 8 to 10 servings.

Cream of Watercress Soup
CRÈME DE CRESSON

4 cups watercress	¼ teaspoon pepper
½ cup chopped onion	2 cans (13¾-ounce size)
2 tablespoons butter or	chicken broth
margarine	1 cup heavy cream
3 tablespoons flour	Watercress for garnish
½ teaspoon salt	

1. Wash watercress thoroughly; drain. Discard coarse stems.

2. In large saucepan, over medium heat, sauté onion in hot butter until golden—about 5 minutes. Remove from heat.

3. Blend in flour, salt, and pepper; slowly stir in chicken broth. Cook, stirring constantly, until mixture comes to boiling and thickens slightly.

4. Add 4 cups watercress; simmer 5 minutes longer. Remove from heat.

5. Blend half of watercress mixture at a time in electric blender 1 minute, or until smooth but still slightly flecked with green.

6. Turn into a large bowl. Add cream. Refrigerate, covered, until well chilled—at least 3 hours.

7. At serving time, garnish with watercress sprigs.

Makes 8 servings.

Cold Cucumber Soup
CRÈME DE CONCOMBRES GLACÉE

3 cucumbers (about 2 pounds)	1 can (13¾ ounces) chicken
3 tablespoons butter or	broth
margarine	1 cup milk
2 tablespoons flour	1 cup light cream
½ teaspoon salt	

1. Pare cucumbers; cut in half lengthwise. With teaspoon, scoop out and discard seeds. Cut cucumber into ¼-inch pieces.

2. In large saucepan, sauté cucumber in hot butter 5 minutes, or until transparent. Remove from heat. Stir in flour and salt until blended. Gradually add chicken broth and milk.

3. Cook over medium heat, stirring constantly, until mixture boils. Reduce heat; simmer, covered, 15 minutes.

4. Turn into electric blender container; blend, at high speed, 1 minute. (Or put mixture through a sieve, pressing cucumber through.) Turn into a bowl.

5. Stir in cream. Refrigerate, covered, until very well chilled—at least 4 hours.

6. Serve in bouillon cups. Garnish with a slice of cucumber if you wish. Makes 8 to 10 servings.

Mediterranean Fish Stew

BOUILLABAISSE

¼ cup olive or salad oil	¼ teaspoon fennel seed
1 cup chopped onion	⅛ teaspoon dried thyme leaves
3 cloves garlic, crushed	⅛ teaspoon pepper
4 bottles (8-ounce size) clam juice	2 bay leaves
2 cans (1-pound, 12-ounce size) whole peeled tomatoes, undrained	2 packages (8-ounce size) frozen rock-lobster tails
	1 pound cod steaks
¾ cup water	1 pound halibut steaks
1 teaspoon grated orange peel	½ pound sea scallops
¾ teaspoon salt	
¼ teaspoon crumbled saffron	1 loaf French bread, thinly sliced and toasted or fried

1. Heat olive oil in an 8-quart kettle. Add chopped onion and the garlic; sauté until the onion is tender—about 5 minutes.

2. Add clam juice, tomatoes with their liquid, ¾ cup water, the orange peel, salt, saffron, fennel seed, thyme, pepper, and bay leaves; bring to boiling. Reduce heat, and simmer mixture, covered, 30 minutes.

3. Remove from heat, and let mixture cool. Then refrigerate, covered, overnight.

4. Next day, cut the lobster tails (shell and all) in half crosswise. Wipe the cod and halibut steaks with damp paper towels. Cut into 1½-inch pieces. Rinse the sea scallops in running cold water, and drain.

5. About 20 minutes before serving, bring tomato mixture just to boiling. Add the lobster; simmer, covered, 4 minutes. Add the cod and

halibut pieces; simmer, covered, 10 minutes. Then add the sea scallops, and cook over low heat for 5 minutes, or just until the scallops are tender.

6. Spoon seafood and broth into soup tureen. Serve bouillabaisse with thin slices of toasted French bread.

Makes 8 servings.

Note: Since this dish calls for many fish found only in the Mediterranean, substitutions have been made. These fish and shellfish may be used also: crab; perch; red or gray snappers; rock, calico, or sea bass; flounder.

Onion Soup

SOUPE À L'OIGNON

¼ cup butter or margarine	4 to 6 slices French bread,
4 cups thinly sliced onion	1 inch thick
4 cans (10½-ounce size)	¼ cup grated Gruyère cheese
condensed beef bouillon,	2 tablespoons grated Parmesan
undiluted	cheese

1. In butter in large skillet, sauté onion until golden, not browned—about 8 minutes.

2. In medium saucepan, combine the bouillon and sautéed onion; bring to boiling. Reduce heat, and simmer, covered, 30 minutes.

3. Meanwhile, in broiler, toast French bread on both sides. Sprinkle each slice with grated cheeses, dividing evenly. Broil just until cheese is bubbly—about 1 minute.

4. To serve: Pour soup into a tureen or individual soup bowls. Float toast, cheese side up, on top.

Makes 4 to 6 servings.

Note: Flavor is enhanced if soup is refrigerated, covered, overnight and reheated at serving time.

Springtime Soup

POTAGE PRINTANIER

2 tablespoons butter or	2 potatoes, pared, quartered,
margarine	and thinly sliced
2 leeks, chopped (about 1 cup)	2 medium carrots, pared and
1 small onion, chopped	thinly sliced
1½ quarts hot water	2 teaspoons salt

¼ cup raw regular white rice
8 stalks fresh or frozen
   asparagus, cut into ½-inch
   pieces

½ pound spinach, washed and
   chopped
1 cup light cream

1. Melt butter in a 3-quart kettle. Add leeks and onion; cook over low heat, covered, about 5 minutes.

2. Add hot water, potato, carrot, and salt; bring to boiling. Reduce heat; simmer, covered, 15 minutes.

3. Add rice and asparagus; simmer, covered, 25 minutes. Add spinach, and simmer 10 minutes longer.

4. Stir in cream; bring just to boiling.

Makes 8 servings.

Note: Flavor is enhanced if soup is refrigerated, covered, overnight and reheated at serving time.

Hearty Cabbage Soup

SOUPE AU CHOU

1½ pounds piece smoked,
   unprocessed ham
¼ cup finely chopped onion
½ cup diced celery
1 cup diced, pared raw potato

2 cans (13¾ ounces)
   chicken broth
2 cups finely chopped cabbage
1 teaspoon salt
¼ teaspoon pepper

1. In large kettle, combine ham, onion, celery, potato, and chicken broth; bring to boiling. Reduce heat; simmer, covered, 15 minutes.

2. Add cabbage, salt, pepper; bring back to boiling. Reduce heat; simmer, covered, 25 minutes longer. Cut ham into bite-size chunks. Serve hot.

Makes 4 servings.

Hearty Beef and Vegetable Soup

POT-AU-FEU

This soup is traditionally served on Sunday. A French housewife would add a chicken carcass to the pot or would simmer a chicken, to be used in the next day's salad or in filled crêpes, in the soup. The broth and meat and vegetables are often served separately. The broth is drunk first, then the meat and vegetables are served with mustard, freshly grated horseradish, and coarse salt.

1 tablespoon salad oil
5 pound shin beef, with bone
3 quarts water
2 cans (1-pound, 12-ounce size) tomatoes, undrained
1 can (6 ounces) tomato paste
½ small head cabbage, cut into quarters
1 pound potatoes, pared and quartered
4 small carrots, pared and cut into 1-inch pieces
2 stalks celery, cut into 1-inch pieces
2 leeks, cut into 1-inch pieces
3 tablespoons salt
1 tablespoon sugar
12 peppercorns
¼ teaspoon cloves
¼ cup barley

1. In hot oil in very large kettle, brown beef well on all sides. Add 3 quarts water.

2. Stir in all remaining ingredients, except barley; bring to boiling. Reduce heat; simmer, covered, 2 hours.

3. Add barley; simmer, covered, 1 hour longer.

4. Let soup cool; then refrigerate, covered, overnight.

5. Skim fat from surface. Bring to boiling. Reduce heat; simmer, covered, 30 minutes.

6. To serve: Remove beef from soup. Cut meat off bone in large pieces. Stir meat into soup.

Makes about 8 quarts.

Eggs

Eggs are rarely served for breakfast in France, but they form the basis of a variety of luncheon and dinner dishes. Eggs are often included in an hors d'oeuvre selection: Accompanying marinated vegetables and cold, sliced meats will be half a deviled egg or a hard-boiled egg smothered with Russian dressing. This last dish, Oeufs à la Russe, is a favorite simple hors d'oeuvre in France. Another method of preparing eggs, also very French, but much more elegant, is Oeufs en Gelée. The yolk of the boiled egg is still soft and the eggs are chilled in wine-flavored aspic.

Many French lunches are planned around an omelet or a soufflé. Omelet-making is an art in France and it is possible to find a delectable omelet anywhere in the country. Golden with butter and firm on the outside, soft and creamy in the center, omelets make a satisfying meal with bread, a green salad, wine, and fruit or a wedge of Brie or Camembert. Omelets are excellent plain, flavored with fresh herbs, or filled and garnished with whatever the cook fancies and the season dictates. In France, omelets—as do many other dishes—reflect regional specialties: seafood fillings in Normandy, unsmoked ham from Gascony, onions in Lyon, cheese and bacon in Lorraine, tomatoes and garlic in Provence.

There are few dishes as impressive as a soufflé, rising puffed and golden in its dish, hot from the oven. Soufflés are exacting dishes to serve when entertaining, for they must go immediately from oven to table; any delay means that the soufflé will have fallen before it reaches the table. However, no dinner or luncheon guest ever minds adjusting to a soufflé's timing.

In France, soufflés are eaten for lunch with bread, salad, and wine, as are omelets. The thrifty French incorporate leftover vegetables, puréed or minced, in their soufflés. Served alone or with a sauce, soufflés are both delicious and economical to make. For dinner, seafood or fish soufflés are a sophisticated first course, and a soufflé flavored with two kinds of cheese is a superb beginning for a dinner featuring Steak au Poivre. Sweet soufflés will be found in the chapter on desserts.

Eggs in Aspic

OEUFS EN GELÉE

6 eggs	¾ teaspoon salt
2 envelopes unflavored gelatine	Boiling water
2 cans (12½-ounce size)	12 fresh tarragon leaves
chicken consommé	4 tablespoons liver pâté
½ cup sauterne	1 teaspoon heavy cream
1 tablespoon tarragon vinegar	

1. Gently lower eggs into boiling water in medium saucepan. Take pan off heat; cover; let stand 3 to 5 minutes. Cool eggs under cold water to prevent further cooking.

2. Sprinkle gelatine over 1 cup consommé in small saucepan to soften. Stir over low heat to dissolve gelatine. Stir in rest of consommé, the sauterne, vinegar, and salt. Set aside.

3. Pour boiling water over tarragon leaves; drain; then plunge leaves into ice water.

4. Beat pâté with heavy cream until smooth. Place in pastry bag with small star tip.

5. Place 6 (6-ounce) oval molds or custard cups in pan of ice and water. Spoon 1 tablespoon gelatine mixture into each mold. Let stand about 5 minutes, or until gelatine is just set. Then arrange 2 drained tarragon leaves on gelatine in each mold. Pipe liver pâté in little stars or in a ring around the leaves. Cover with another tablespoon of gelatine mixture, being careful to keep decoration intact. Let stand until the gelatine is firm.

6. Meanwhile, carefully peel eggs. Place an egg in center of each mold on firm-gelatine layer. Pour enough gelatine mixture around the eggs just to cover them.

7. Refrigerate molds, along with any remaining gelatine mixture, until firm.

8. To unmold: Dip molds in hot water; invert onto individual serving

plates, and shake gently to release. Garnish with parsley, if desired, and remaining gelatine, chopped.

Makes 6 servings.

Note: The yolks of these eggs should be soft in the center, so be careful not to overcook.

Whipped Cream Omelet 1569776

OMELETTE MOUSSELINE

8 eggs	6 tablespoons butter or
2 tablespoons heavy cream	margarine
Salt and pepper	

1. Separate eggs, placing the whites in a large bowl and the yolks in a medium bowl.

2. With electric beater at high speed, beat the egg whites until stiff peaks form when the beater is slowly raised.

3. With same beater, beat egg yolks well. Beat in cream, ½ teaspoon salt, and dash pepper. Slowly heat an 11-inch skillet. Add butter, and heat until it sizzles—do not brown.

4. Pour in egg yolk mixture. When it begins to set (5 to 10 seconds), add beaten egg whites; quickly fold into yolk mixture with wire whisk or spatula. Cook over medium heat, shaking skillet gently, until omelet is puffy and almost set—takes 3 to 5 minutes.

5. With wide spatula, quickly loosen omelet from side of skillet; tilt skillet, and fold omelet in half. Slip omelet onto serving platter, and serve at once.

Makes 4 servings.

Cheese Soufflé

SOUFFLÉ AU FROMAGE

6 eggs	Dash cayenne
Butter or margarine	1¼ cups milk
Grated Parmesan cheese	½ cup coarsely grated natural
6 tablespoons unsifted	Swiss cheese
all-purpose flour	¼ teaspoon cream of tartar
1½ teaspoons salt	

1. Separate eggs, placing whites in large bowl, yolks in another bowl. Set aside while whites warm to room temperature—about 1 hour.

2. Meanwhile, butter 1½-quart straight-side soufflé dish (7½ inches in diameter). Dust lightly with Parmesan—about 1 tablespoon.

3. Tear off a sheet of waxed paper, 26 inches long. Fold lengthwise into thirds. Lightly butter one side.

4. Wrap waxed paper around soufflé dish, with buttered side against dish and a 2-inch rim extending about edge top. Tie with string.

5. Preheat the oven to 350° F.

6. Melt 5 tablespoons butter in a medium saucepan; remove from heat. Stir in flour, 1 teaspoon salt, and cayenne until smooth. Gradually stir in milk.

7. Bring to boiling, stirring. Reduce heat, and simmer, stirring constantly, until mixture becomes very thick and begins to leave the bottom and sides of pan.

8. With wire whisk or wooden spoon, beat egg yolks. Gradually beat in cooked mixture. Add ½ cup Parmesan cheese and the Swiss cheese; beat until well combined.

9. Add remaining ½ teaspoon salt and the cream of tartar to egg whites. With portable electric mixer at high speed, beat until stiff peaks form when beater is raised.

10. Fold one-third of beaten egg whites into cheese mixture until well combined. Carefully fold in remaining egg whites just until combined. Turn into prepared dish.

11. Bake 40 minutes, or until soufflé is puffed and golden brown. Remove collar. Serve at once.

Makes 4 servings.

Lobster Soufflé, Plaza Athénée

SOUFFLÉ DE HOMARD, PLAZA ATHÉNÉE

Lobster Mixture
3 (1-pound size) live lobsters;*
   or 3 (10- to 12-ounce size)
   frozen rock-lobster tails,
   thawed
¼ cup salad oil

¼ cup finely chopped pared
   carrot
¼ cup finely chopped onion
1 tablespoon chopped parsley
1 tablespoon chopped chives
1 teaspoon paprika

*To kill lobster: Lay lobster on back on wooden board. Sever spinal cord by inserting point of knife through to back shell where body and tail of lobster come together. Then, with sharp knife, split body down middle, cutting through the undershell. Discard dark vein and small sac 2 inches below head. Crack large claws with nutcracker.

1 cup heavy cream
½ cup sauterne
2 tablespoons cognac

Lobster Sauce
3 tablespoons butter or
   margarine
3 tablespoons flour
1 cup milk
¼ cup heavy cream
¼ cup dry sherry

Soufflé
5 tablespoons butter or
   margarine
6 tablespoons flour
2 teaspoons salt
Cayenne
1¼ cups milk
6 egg yolks, beaten
½ cup grated Parmesan cheese
6 egg whites, at room
   temperature
½ teaspoon cream of tartar

1. Prepare Lobster Mixture: With sharp knife, cut lobster and shell into large pieces (if using tails, cut into thirds). In hot oil in large skillet, sauté lobster pieces (shell and all), turning occasionally, 5 minutes, or until red. Remove to bowl.

2. In drippings in same skillet, sauté carrot, onion, parsley, and chives until carrot and onion are tender—about 2 minutes.

3. Return lobster to skillet. Add paprika, 1 cup cream, the sauterne, and cognac; cook gently, covered, 10 minutes.

4. Remove lobster; cut away shell and discard. Slice lobster meat ¼ inch thick; set aside.

5. Over medium heat, simmer the cream mixture, stirring, to reduce to 1 cup. Force through coarse strainer. Reserve for Lobster Sauce.

6. Make Lobster Sauce: Melt 3 tablespoons butter in small saucepan. Remove from heat; stir in 3 tablespoons flour until smooth. Gradually stir in 1 cup milk.

7. Bring to boiling, stirring. Remove from heat; stir in cream, sherry, and reserved mixture.

8. Combine 1 cup sauce with cut-up lobster. Turn into 1½-quart shallow baking dish. Reserve rest of sauce.

9. Preheat oven to 375°F.

10. Make Soufflé: Melt butter in medium saucepan. Remove from heat; stir in flour, 1 teaspoon salt, and dash cayenne until smooth. Gradually stir in milk.

11. Bring to boiling, stirring. Then reduce heat; simmer until mixture becomes very thick and leaves bottom and sides of pan. Remove from heat.

12. With wire whisk, beat mixture into egg yolks in large bowl; mix well. Beat in cheese.

13. In large bowl, with electric mixer at high speed, beat egg whites with cream of tartar and 1 teaspoon salt just until stiff peaks form when beater is slowly raised.

14. With wire whisk or rubber scraper, fold egg whites, one half at a time, into egg yolk mixture just until well combined. Pour over lobster in baking dish.

15. Bake 35 to 40 minutes, or until puffed and nicely browned. Just before serving, gently reheat reserved lobster sauce. Serve soufflé at once, with sauce.

Makes 6 servings.

Fish

The French eat a great deal of seafood, both fresh and salt water. The seafood is always impeccably fresh and well prepared. Fish is cooked with care—a cook would never serve broken fillets or raggedly sliced lobster tail—and subtly sauced. It is with the combination of delicate seafood and complementary sauces that one can truly see the skill of French cuisine in the pairing of meat and sauce so that neither loses its individuality, yet all the flavors blend together.

In France fish is often poached and then sauced, with the sauce based on the poaching liquid, which is usually white wine but may be fish stock or lemon-flavored court bouillon. Fish is never cooked in plain water. The classic sauces for fish often include a garnish of several kinds of shellfish—scallops, shrimp, lobster, mussels, or the plentiful and popular freshwater crayfish, écrevisse. For instance, lobster flavors the sauce of quenelles, a light and delicate fish dumpling that is a distinguished first course, and shrimp and oysters decorate Filets de Sole Marguéry. Shellfish themselves also form the basis of many of France's most delicious seafood dishes like Mussels Steamed in Wine and Scallops in White Wine Sauce.

Many of the seafood dishes prepared in France have a regional flavor. Shellfish dishes are more commonly eaten along the Atlantic and Mediterranean coasts, while trout is found inland where it goes from brook to pan in as short a time as possible. Frogs' legs also come from the inland streams and ponds. The sole caught on the Atlantic coast is particularly fine, and Normandy is known for its method of preparing sole with a mussel garnish. Bouillabaisse (*see* page 29 for recipe) is one of the most famous dishes of the Mediterranean; flavored with saffron, tomatoes, garlic, and olive oil—the tastes of the south of France—it is made in every French kitchen that has access to the necessary shellfish and fish. Another popular fish in Provence is bourride, poached white fish with garlic mayonnaise. Firm fish like mullet are broiled here over dried fennel branches, which gives them an incomparable flavor.

The recipes in this chapter can be served as the main course for dinner or lunch, or as a first course. Particularly good as first courses are Mussels Steamed in Wine, Coquilles St. Jacques, Quenelles with Lobster Sauce, and the simply prepared fillets of fish.

All fish cookery is improved if gros sal, sea salt, sold either coarse or milled at health food stores, is used instead of table salt for flavoring.

Mussels Steamed in Wine

MOULES À LA MARINIÈRE

3 dozen mussels	½ cup chopped parsley
1½ cups chopped onion	⅛ teaspoon pepper
1 clove garlic, crushed	Pinch dried thyme leaves
⅓ cup butter or margarine	2 tablespoons soft butter or
2 cups Chablis	margarine
2 tablespoons lemon juice	1 teaspoon flour

1. Check mussels, discarding any that are not tightly closed. Scrub well under cold running water, to remove sand and seaweed. With a sharp knife, trim off the "beard" around edges. Place mussels in large bowl: Cover with cold water. Let soak 1 to 2 hours.

2. Lift mussels from water, and place in a colander. Rinse with cold water; let drain.

3. In 6-quart kettle, sauté onion and garlic in ⅓ cup butter until golden and tender—about 10 minutes. Add wine, lemon juice, ¼ cup parsley, the pepper, and thyme; bring to boiling. Add mussels; cook over high heat, covered, 5 to 8 minutes, or until shells open. Shake kettle frequently, so mussels will cook uniformly.

4. With slotted utensil, remove mussels to heated serving dish. Cover with hot, damp cloth.

5. Quickly return cooking liquid to boiling; boil, uncovered, until reduced to about 2 cups—about 5 minutes. Mix soft butter with flour until

smooth. Stir into boiling liquid, and cook, stirring, 2 minutes longer. Taste and add salt if needed.

6. Spoon sauce over mussels: sprinkle with remaining parsley. Serve immediately.

Makes 3 or 4 main-dish servings, 6 appetizer servings.

Scallops in White Wine Sauce

COQUILLES ST. JACQUES

1 teaspoon lemon juice	1 cup light cream
½ teaspoon salt	½ cup milk
2 pounds sea scallops, washed and drained	1 cup grated Gruyère cheese
	½ cup dry white wine
4 tablespoons butter or margarine	1 tablespoon lemon juice
	1 tablespoon chopped parsley
¼ cup finely chopped onion	
¼ pound mushrooms, sliced; or 1 can (3 ounces) sliced mushrooms, drained	½ cup packaged dry bread crumbs
	2 tablespoons butter or margarine, melted
⅓ cup flour	
Dash pepper	

1. In medium saucepan, combine 1 cup water, 1 teaspoon lemon juice, and the salt; bring to boiling. Add scallops; simmer, covered, 6 minutes, or till tender. Drain on paper towels.

2. In 4 tablespoons hot butter in medium saucepan, sauté onion and mushrooms until tender—about 5 minutes. Remove from heat; stir in flour and pepper until well blended. Gradually stir in cream and milk.

3. Bring to boiling, stirring. Reduce heat, and simmer, stirring frequently, until quite thick—4 to 5 minutes. Add cheese, and stir until melted. Remove from heat.

4. Carefully stir in wine, lemon juice, and parsley. Then add scallops. Turn into 8 scallop shells or a 1½-quart casserole.

5. Mix bread crumbs and melted butter; sprinkle over scallops. Place shells on cookie sheet.

6. Broil, 4 inches from heat, until golden brown—2 to 3 minutes.

Makes 8 servings.

Lobster Thermidor

HOMARD THERMIDOR

8 frozen rock-lobster tails
  (3 pounds)
3 tablespoons sherry
2 tablespoons brandy

Sauce
½ cup butter or margarine
¼ cup unsifted all-purpose flour

1 teaspoon salt
⅛ teaspoon mace
Dash paprika
1½ cups light cream
1 egg yolk, slightly beaten
½ cup grated sharp Cheddar
  cheese

1. Cook frozen lobster tails as package label directs. Drain; cool quickly in cold water; drain.

2. Remove lobster meat from shells, keeping shells intact. Cut lobster into bite-size pieces.

3. In large bowl, toss lobster with sherry and brandy; cover; set aside.

4. Wash and dry lobster shells; set aside.

5. Preheat oven to 450°F.

6. Make Sauce: Melt butter in large saucepan; remove from heat. Stir in flour, salt, mace, and paprika. Gradually stir in cream.

7. Bring to boiling, stirring constantly; reduce heat, and simmer several minutes.

8. Stir some of hot mixture into egg yolk; pour back into saucepan. Add lobster meat.

9. Cook, stirring, over low heat, until sauce is thickened and lobster is heated through.

10. With shells arranged on cookie sheet, fill them with lobster mixture, mounding high. Sprinkle each with 1 tablespoon grated cheese.

11. Bake until cheese is melted and top is golden-brown—8 to 10 minutes.

Makes 8 servings.

Fresh Fish Quenelles with Lobster Sauce

QUENELLES DE BROCHET

Quenelles
1 cup water
1 cup butter or margarine
Salt
1 cup unsifted all-purpose flour

2 eggs
2 egg whites
1 tablespoon prepared hot
  mustard
¼ teaspoon mace

Green Salad

Baba au Rhum

Tournedos with Béarnaise Sauce

Crêpes Suzette

¼ teaspoon white pepper   1 egg yolk
1 pound pike or halibut fillets,
    ground*   Lobster Sauce, page 76
¼ cup heavy cream   Mushroom caps for garnish

1 package (8 ounces)
    refrigerator crescent rolls

1. Day before, make Quenelles: In medium saucepan, bring 1 cup water with ¼ cup butter and ¼ teaspoon salt slowly to boiling.

2. Remove from heat. With wooden spoon, beat in the flour all at once, beating until smooth. Return to low heat; continue beating 2 minutes.

3. Turn mixture into large bowl of electric mixer. At high speed, beat in, one at a time, eggs and whites, beating until smooth. Beat in mustard, mace, pepper, 1 tablespoon salt.

4. Gradually add ground fish, a tablespoon at a time, beating well after each addition and scraping beaters and side of bowl.

5. Turn mixture into another bowl. In large mixer bowl, cream remaining butter until light. Slowly add fish mixture, beating constantly.

6. Beat in heavy cream gradually.

7. Turn mixture into a shallow glass baking dish, spreading evenly. Refrigerate, covered, overnight.

8. Next day, preheat oven to 375°F. Make crescents: Separate dough into 8 triangles. Mix egg yolk with 1 tablespoon water; brush over 4 triangles. Top with other triangles.

9. Using a 3-inch crescent cookie cutter, cut 8 crescents. Place on ungreased cookie sheet; brush with yolk.

10. Bake 10 to 13 minutes, or until deep golden. Keep warm. (Trimmings can also be baked.)

11. In a large, deep skillet, bring 1½ inches water to simmering.

12. Using a number-24 small ice-cream scoop or about 2 heaping tablespoons for each, shape quenelles into cylinders about 2½ inches long and 1 inch wide. Cook, uncovered, in water 15 minutes, turning once.

13. Lift out with slotted spoon; place in serving dish. Keep warm.

14. Pour Lobster Sauce over all. Garnish with crescents and sautéed mushrooms.

Makes 6 servings.

Use fresh (not frozen) fish. Put raw fish through medium blade of food chopper or food mill.

Grilled Fish Provençal

POISSON GRILLÉ À LA PROVENÇALE

4 pounds whole striped bass, dressed and split	1½ teaspoons chopped fresh thyme leaves*
4 tablespoons salad or olive oil	2 tablespoons chopped fresh tarragon leaves*
4 tablespoons lemon juice	1 teaspoon chopped fresh rosemary leaves*
1½ teaspoons salt	1 small onion, sliced
¼ teaspoon pepper	Chopped parsley
1 small stalk celery with leaves, chopped	Lemon wedges

1. Wash fish thoroughly; pat dry inside and out with paper towels.

2. With sharp knife, make 4 diagonal slashes through skin on each side.

3. In small bowl, combine oil and lemon juice. Brush some of mixture over inside of fish; sprinkle with 1 teaspoon salt and the pepper.

4. In small bowl, combine celery, thyme, tarragon, and rosemary. Sprinkle half of mixture over inside of fish; add onion slices in a layer; sprinkle with remaining herb mixture. Close opening with skewers.

5. Add rest of salt to remaining oil mixture. Brush some of mixture over both sides of fish.

6. Place fish on a well-oiled grill or in basket, and adjust 5 inches above prepared coals. Cook 15 to 20 minutes, or until fish flakes easily when tested with a fork on underside. Brush with remaining oil mixture. Carefully turn fish with wide spatulas, or turn basket; cook 15 to 20 minutes, or until done.

7. Remove to serving platter. Sprinkle with parsley; garnish with lemon wedges.

Makes 6 servings.

Halibut Mornay

POISSON À LA MORNAY

2½ pounds halibut fillets	⅛ teaspoon pepper
5 tablespoons butter or margarine	1 bay leaf
Salt	½ cup water
	1 cup milk

*Or use ½ teaspoon dried thyme, 2 teaspoons dried tarragon, and ¼ teaspoon dried rosemary.

3 whole black peppers	2 tablespoons flour
1 tablespoon finely chopped onion	½ cup grated Parmesan cheese

1. Wash halibut; dry on paper towels. If very large, cut into serving-size pieces.

2. Melt 2 tablespoons butter in large skillet. Add fish, 1 teaspoon salt, the pepper, bay leaf, and ½ cup water. Bring to boiling; reduce heat, and simmer, covered, 15 minutes, or just until fish flakes easily with fork.

3. Meanwhile, place milk, black peppers, and onion in small saucepan; bring to boiling. Remove from heat.

4. Drain fish well, reserving ½ cup liquid. Discard bay leaf. Arrange fish in heatproof serving dish.

5. Melt remaining butter in same skillet; remove from heat. Stir in flour and ¼ teaspoon salt until smooth. Gradually stir in warm milk mixture and reserved fish liquid.

6. Cook over medium heat, stirring, until thickened. Add ¼ cup Parmesan; cook, stirring, until cheese is melted. Pour over fish. Sprinkle remaining Parmesan over top.

7. Run under broiler 3 to 5 minutes, or until cheese is golden brown. Makes 6 servings.

Broiled Salmon Steaks with Tarragon Butter

SAUMON GRILLÉ, BEURRE D'ESTRAGON

Marinade	Dash pepper
½ cup lemon juice	4 (6- to 8-ounce size) salmon
1 tablespoon dried tarragon leaves	steaks, ¾ inch thick
¼ teaspoon salt	About 2 tablespoons butter or margarine

1. Make Marinade: In shallow dish, combine lemon juice, tarragon, salt, and pepper.

2. Wash salmon steaks; dry with paper towels. Place in marinade, turning to coat both sides. Refrigerate, covered, about 1½ hours; turn steaks once or twice.

3. Remove steaks from marinade, and arrange on rack in broiler pan. Reserve marinade. Top each steak with a thin pat of butter.

4. Broil, 4 inches from heat, 5 minutes. Turn steaks; brush with marinade, and top with a thin pat of butter. Broil 5 to 8 minutes longer, or until fish flakes easily with fork.

Makes 4 servings.

Fillets of Sole with Mushrooms

FILETS DE SOLE BONNE FEMME

6 fillets of sole (2½ to 3
   pounds)
¾ teaspoon salt
⅛ teaspoon pepper
5 tablespoons butter or
   margarine
½ cup water
¼ cup dry white wine
1 small onion, sliced
1 bay leaf
3 tablespoons flour
Dash cayenne
¼ cup light cream

Sautéed Mushrooms:
2 tablespoons butter or
   margarine
½ cup sliced mushrooms or 1 can
   (3 ounces) sliced mushrooms,
   drained
½ teaspoon lemon juice
Dash salt
Dash cayenne

Hollandaise Sauce, page 71

1. Preheat oven to 350°F. Gently wash sole fillets; pat dry with paper towels.

2. Arrange the sole fillets in a buttered shallow roasting pan. Sprinkle with ¾ teaspoon salt and ⅛ teaspoon pepper; dot with 2 tablespoons butter or margarine. Pour ½ cup water and the white wine over all. Top the sole with the sliced onion and the bay leaf.

3. Bake, uncovered, 15 minutes, or until the fish flakes easily when tested with a fork.

4. Remove onion and bay leaf. Then carefully remove sole to heat-resistant serving platter; keep warm. Strain fish stock, and set aside until ready to use.

5. Melt 3 tablespoons butter in small saucepan. Remove from heat. Stir in flour and dash cayenne until smooth. Gradually stir in fish stock (it should measure 1¼ cups). Bring to boiling, stirring constantly. Reduce heat, and simmer 3 minutes. Stir in light cream; mix well. Pour sauce over sole.

6. Meanwhile, prepare the Sautéed Mushrooms: In hot butter in skillet, sauté the sliced mushrooms with lemon juice, salt, and cayenne until they are golden brown. Also, make Hollandaise Sauce.

7. Spoon sautéed mushrooms over sole. Then spoon hollandaise sauce over mushrooms.

8. Broil, 4 inches from heat, until nicely browned on top. If desired, garnish platter with a few sautéed mushroom caps and fresh tarragon sprigs.

Makes 6 servings.

Sole with Shrimp and Oysters
FILETS DE SOLE MARGUÉRY

6 sole, haddock, or flounder
  fillets (about 2½ pounds)
6 onion rings
½ cup water
½ cup sauterne or chablis
1 bay leaf
3 whole black peppers
1 dozen raw shrimp, shelled
  and deveined

1 dozen fresh oysters

3 tablespoons butter or margarine
2 tablespoons flour
½ teaspoon salt
⅛ teaspoon pepper
2 tablespoons heavy cream

1. Preheat oven to 400°F. Lightly grease 13-by-9-by-1¾-inch baking dish. Wash fillets; dry on paper towels.

2. Fold fillets in half crosswise, and place in prepared baking dish. Top each with an onion ring. Add ½ cup water, the sauterne, bay leaf, and black peppers.

3. Cover dish with foil; bake 20 minutes, or just until fish flakes easily with fork. Do not overcook the fish.

4. Meanwhile, place shrimp, oysters, and 1 cup water in medium saucepan; bring to boiling. Reduce heat, and simmer, covered, 5 minutes. Drain, and set aside.

5. Carefully remove fish from baking dish, discarding onion rings, and drain well. Strain liquid, and reserve 1 cup.

6. Arrange fillets in heatproof serving dish, or return to baking dish, with shrimp and oysters; keep warm.

7. Melt 2 tablespoons butter in small saucepan; remove from heat. Stir in flour, salt, and pepper until smooth. Gradually stir in reserved fish liquid. Cook over medium heat, stirring, until thickened. Stir in cream.

8. Pour sauce over fish. Melt remaining butter, and pour over sauce. Run under broiler 3 to 5 minutes, or until golden brown.

Makes 6 servings.

Fillets of Sole in White Wine
FILETS DE SOLE AU VIN BLANC

1 bottle (7½ ounces) clam juice
½ cup dry white wine
½ bay leaf
6 whole black peppers
½ teaspoon salt
Sprig of fresh dill or parsley
1 clove garlic, split

½ cup water
2 pounds fillets of sole
Lemon juice

White Wine Sauce, page 75
Chopped parsley

1. In 2-quart saucepan, combine clam juice, white wine, bay leaf, black peppers, salt, dill, garlic, and ½ cup water; bring to boiling. Reduce heat, and simmer, uncovered, for 15 minutes. Set the mixture aside.

2. Preheat the oven to 350°F.

3. Wipe fillets of sole with damp paper towels. Sprinkle with lemon juice. Fold each fillet into thirds (the darker side inside). Arrange the fillets in a single layer in a shallow baking dish.

4. Strain clam mixture over fillets. Cover dish tightly with foil. Poach fish in oven 15 minutes. Drain fillets; strain liquid, and reserve 1 cup for White Wine Sauce. Keep fillets warm on serving platter.

5. Make White Wine Sauce. Pour over fillets. Sprinkle with chopped parsley.

Makes 4 to 6 servings.

Poultry

Poultry, particularly chicken, lends itself well to a number of methods of preparation. Chicken can be magnificent either simply roasted or served with a traditional sauce that takes hours to prepare. Because of its versatility and its own good flavor, chicken has always been a favorite of the French. Chicken is often served for Sunday dinner, either perfectly roasted and without stuffing, poached with vegetables, or stewed in a savory wine sauce. Chicken naturally adapts to regional dishes like a chicken stew from Normandy, where cider is used instead of wine for the liquid. Suprêmes, skinned and boned breasts of chicken, are found in numerous recipes.

Several areas of France are noted for the particularly succulent chickens that they raise, and one of the most famous is the Bresse chicken from Lyon. French chickens have a good deal more flavor than the birds that are available in American supermarkets. An American cook will find that it is worth buying the usually more expensive but certainly fresher and more flavorful chicken the local butcher carries. In preparing chicken, the French never wash them before cooking as Americans do, believing that it harms the flavor and hastens spoilage.

Duckling is also a favorite French meal. Although only one size of duckling, almost always sold frozen, is available in America, the French can choose from three different ducks: the nantais, the youngest and most popular duckling, the rouennais, usually reserved for pressed duck, and the canard de barbarie, most often used in stews. The degree of doneness a duck is cooked is important to the French; the duck must be à point, neither underdone or overdone. Wild duck is traditionally served rare.

Goose is raised for its superb liver, foie gras, the best of which comes from Alsace and the southwestern region of France around Toulouse, and for roasting. Goose meat, preserved in its own fat, is a traditional ingredient in cassoulet in Languedoc.

Poached Chicken with Vegetables

POULET EN CASSEROLE

4- to 5-pound ready-to-cook roasting chicken, with giblets	1½ pounds small new potatoes, pared
Salt	¼ cup butter or margarine, melted
⅛ teaspoon pepper	4 teaspoons flour
¼ cup butter or margarine	½ cup dry white wine
8 leeks	½ cup canned chicken broth
1½ to 2 pounds small carrots, pared	2 bunches chives
	Chopped parsley

1. Remove giblets from chicken; rinse giblets, and set aside on paper towels. Rinse chicken well; dry with paper towels. Sprinkle inside with 1½ teaspoons salt and the pepper. Tuck wings under body; tie legs together. If necessary, fasten skin at neck with a skewer.

2. In ¼ cup hot butter in Dutch oven, brown chicken well all over—takes about 30 minutes. Turn chicken carefully with two wooden spoons; do not break skin.

3. Meanwhile, coarsely chop giblets. Wash leeks well; cut off roots, and discard. Remove some of top leaves, and add to giblets. Then halve leeks crosswise, and set aside.

4. Place giblet-leek mixture under browned chicken. Cover tightly, and simmer over low heat 30 minutes.

5. Arrange carrots (halved, if necessary) around the chicken; simmer, covered, 40 minutes longer, or until chicken and carrots are tender. Remove from heat.

6. Meanwhile, cook potatoes in 1 inch boiling salted water in medium saucepan, covered, 20 to 25 minutes, or until tender. Drain; then drizzle with 2 tablespoons melted butter.

7. Also, cook halved leeks in 1 inch boiling water in medium saucepan, covered, 10 minutes, or until tender. Drain, and drizzle with 2 tablespoons melted butter.

8. Carefully remove chicken and carrots to heated platter; keep warm.

9. Strain drippings; return to Dutch oven. Stir in flour until smooth. Gradually stir in wine and chicken broth; bring to boiling. Reduce heat, and simmer 3 minutes. Taste, and add salt, if needed.

10. To serve: Arrange potatoes, leeks, and bunches of chives around chicken and carrots. Sprinkle potatoes with parsley. Pass gravy.

Makes 4 to 6 servings.

Chicken in Red Wine
COQ AU VIN

2½-pound broiler-fryer, quartered	2½ tablespoons flour
6 slices bacon, diced	1 teaspoon salt
2 tablespoons butter or margarine	¼ teaspoon dried thyme leaves
8 whole mushrooms	⅛ teaspoon pepper
8 small white onions, peeled	2 cups Burgundy
⅔ cup sliced green onion	1 cup canned condensed chicken broth, undiluted
1 clove garlic, crushed	8 small new potatoes, scrubbed
	Chopped parsley

1. Wash the chicken; dry on paper towels.

2. In Dutch oven, sauté bacon until crisp. Remove. Add butter to drippings; heat. Add chicken, and brown well all over. Remove.

3. Pour off all but 2 tablespoons fat from Dutch oven. Add mushrooms and white onions to Dutch oven; cook until nicely browned. Remove; set aside with chicken.

4. Add green onion and garlic to Dutch oven; sauté 2 minutes. Remove from heat. Stir in flour, salt, thyme, and pepper. Return to heat, and cook, stirring constantly, until the flour is browned—takes 3 minutes.

5. Gradually stir in Burgundy and chicken broth; bring to boiling, stirring. Remove from heat. Add bacon, chicken, onions, and mushrooms and stir. Refrigerate, covered, overnight. Next day, preheat oven to 400°F. Add the scrubbed potatoes to chicken mixture.

6. Bake, covered, about 1 hour and 50 minutes, or until chicken and potatoes are tender. Garnish with parsley.

Makes 4 servings.

Chicken Marengo

POULET À LA MARENGO

1 (2½-pound) broiler-fryer, cut up
2 tablespoons salad oil
1 medium onion, peeled and quartered
1 tablespoon flour
1 cup canned chicken broth
¼ cup tomato paste
¼ cup dry white wine
Chopped parsley
½ teaspoon salt

¼ teaspoon dried marjoram leaves
¼ teaspoon pepper
1 clove garlic, crushed
½ bay leaf
1 package (6 ounces) frozen mushrooms; or 1 can (6 ounces) whole mushrooms, drained
1 medium tomato, cut into thin wedges
½ teaspoon sugar

1. Wipe chicken with damp paper towels.

2. Heat oil in large, heavy skillet. Brown chicken, a few pieces at a time, turning on all sides. Remove chicken as it browns.

3. In drippings in skillet, sauté onion 2 minutes.

4. Remove from heat; stir in flour until well combined. Gradually add chicken broth; add tomato paste, wine, 1 tablespoon chopped parsley, the salt, marjoram, pepper, garlic, and bay leaf; stir to blend well.

5. Add chicken and mushrooms to sauce. Place tomato wedges over top of chicken; sprinkle with sugar; simmer, covered, until chicken is tender—about 35 minutes.

6. With slotted spoon, remove chicken and tomato wedges to a heated platter.

7. Spoon sauce over and around chicken. Sprinkle with parsley.
Makes 4 to 6 servings.

Chicken Normandy

POULET SAUTÉ À LA NORMANDE

3- pound broiler-fryer, cut up
¼ cup unsifted all-purpose flour
1 teaspoon seasoned salt
¼ teaspoon pepper
3 tablespoons salad oil
1 clove garlic, peeled
1 large onion, sliced

1 green pepper, cut into ¼-inch strips
¼ teaspoon nutmeg
1½ cups apple cider
1 large tart apple
2 tablespoons brown sugar
2 lemon slices

1. Rinse chicken pieces well in cold running water; dry the chicken pieces well on several thicknesses of paper towels.

2. Combine all-purpose flour, the seasoned salt, and pepper in a paper bag; mix well. Then add the chicken pieces to bag; shake well to coat chicken all over with flour mixture.

3. In some of the hot oil in large skillet, sauté garlic for a few minutes, until it is golden. Remove and discard garlic.

4. Using tongs, remove chicken pieces as they brown. Add sliced onion and green pepper strips to drippings in skillet; sauté vegetables until tender—about five minutes or longer.

5. Return chicken to the skillet; sprinkle with the nutmeg. Add 1 cup cider; cook the chicken, covered, over medium heat, about 20 minutes.

6. Pare apple; core; cut into ¼-inch-thick slices.

7. Add remaining ½ cup cider. Arrange sliced apple over top of chicken; sprinkle top of chicken and sliced apple with brown sugar; arrange the lemon slices over all.

8. Bring to boiling; reduce heat, and simmer, covered, 30 minutes, or until the chicken and apple slices are tender. Taste for seasoning, and add salt and pepper, if necessary.

9. Serve chicken with apples and sauce from skillet spooned over. Serve with parsleyed rice.

Makes 4 servings.

Chicken Breasts in White Wine

SUPRÊMES DE VOLAILLE AU VIN BLANC

12 whole chicken breasts, split (about 10 pounds)	½ teaspoon salt
	½ teaspoon pepper
½ pound butter or margarine	½ teaspoon dried thyme leaves
2 cups finely chopped onion	2 cans (13¾-ounce size)
½ pound small mushrooms, washed	chicken broth
	4 chicken bouillon cubes
2 cloves garlic, crushed	2 cups sauterne
½ cup unsifted all-purpose flour	

1. Wash chicken breasts; dry on paper towels. Remove skin.

2. In some of hot butter in a 5-quart Dutch oven with tight-fitting lid, gently brown chicken breasts, a few at a time; add more butter as needed. Remove chicken breasts as they brown. Continue until all chicken is browned.

3. Add onion, mushrooms, and garlic; sauté, stirring, about 5 minutes. Remove from heat.

4. Combine flour with salt, pepper and thyme. Stir into onion mixture.

5. Gradually stir in chicken broth; crumble in bouillon cubes.

6. Bring to boiling, stirring; reduce heat, and add sauterne.

7. Preheat oven to 400°F.

8. Add chicken breasts to wine mixture; bake, covered, 30 minutes.

9. To freeze: Divide chicken mixture into thirds. Place each third (8 servings) in a foil-lined 2-quart casserole; fold foil over chicken. Freeze until solid. Then remove foil package from casserole, and overwrap in freezer-wrapping material. Seal; label; return to freezer.

10. To serve: Remove overwrap and foil from packages of frozen chicken, according to number of servings desired. Place each 8-serving package in a 2-quart casserole; bake in 400°F oven, covered, 40 minutes; stir; bake 15 minutes, or until bubbly. Garnish with parsley.

Makes 24 servings in all.

Breast of Chicken Parisienne

SUPRÊMES DE VOLAILLE À LA PARISIENNE

½ ounce dried mushrooms	1 teaspoon catsup
3 whole chicken breasts, split, boned, and skinned (1¾ pounds in all)	½ teaspoon meat-extract paste*
	⅛ teaspoon salt
	Dash cayenne
¼ cup butter or margarine	1 cup canned condensed chicken broth, undiluted
2 tablespoons brandy	
2 tablespoons finely chopped onion	½ cup light cream
	Sprig fresh tarragon
¼ teaspoon finely chopped garlic	2 fresh mushrooms, very thinly sliced
2 tablespoons flour	2 teaspoons tarragon vinegar

1. Soak dried mushrooms as package label directs; then drain and finely chop. Wash chicken, and pat dry with paper towels.

2. Heat butter in large skillet. Add chicken, and brown on each side—4 minutes a side.

3. Heat brandy in small saucepan: ignite with match and pour over chicken. Remove chicken, and set aside.

Do not use liquid meat extract.

4. Add chopped mushrooms, onion, and garlic; cook over low heat a few minutes. Remove from heat.

5. Stir in flour, catsup, meat-extract paste, salt, and cayenne until well blended. Gradually stir in chicken broth and ⅓ cup cream; bring to boiling, stirring constantly.

6. Return chicken to skillet. Add tarragon and sliced mushrooms; simmer, covered, 25 to 30 minutes, or until chicken is tender. Remove chicken to heated platter.

7. Stir remaining cream and the tarragon vinegar into sauce. Pour over chicken.

Makes 6 servings.

Duckling with Turnips

CANETON AUX NAVETS

5-pound ready-to-cook duckling	1 can (10½ ounces) condensed
1 teaspoon salt	chicken broth, undiluted
3 tablespoons butter or	½ cup white wine
margarine	Pinch dried thyme leaves
1 medium onion, sliced	3 tablespoons flour
1 small white turnip, pared and	
diced	Glazed Onions and Turnips,
1 sprig parsley	page 83
	Chopped parsley

1. Preheat oven to 425°F. Sprinkle duckling inside and out with salt. Tie ends of legs together. Prick skin all over with fork. Place, breast side up, on a rack in shallow roasting pan.

2. Roast, uncovered, 45 minutes, or until nicely browned.

3. Meanwhile, in 1 tablespoon hot butter, sauté onion, turnip, and parsley sprig until golden—about 10 minutes. Set aside.

4. Remove duckling from oven. Prick skin all over again. Reduce oven temperature to 350°F. Pour all fat from pan, and discard. Arrange sautéed vegetables around duckling. Add chicken broth, wine, and thyme. Cover pan with foil.

5. Roast, covered, 1 hour longer, or until tender. Pour off all pan juices, and strain into a 4-cup measure; skim off fat. Add more wine to juices, if necessary, to make 2 cups. Raise oven temperature to 400°F. Return duckling to oven, uncovered, for 15 minutes, to crisp skin.

6. Melt 2 tablespoons butter in saucepan; remove from heat. Stir in flour until smooth. Gradually stir in pan juices; bring to boiling, stirring constantly. Reduce heat, and simmer 3 minutes.

7. To serve: Arrange duckling and glazed vegetables on heated platter. Garnish with chopped parsley. Pass sauce.

Makes 4 servings.

Orange-glazed Roast Duckling

CANETON À L'ORANGE

4- to 5-pound ready-to-cook duckling, quartered	½ cup white wine
1 teaspoon salt	2 large navel oranges
2 tablespoons flour	½ cup orange juice
1 can (10½ ounces) condensed chicken broth, undiluted	⅓ cup sugar
	⅓ cup light corn syrup
	2 tablespoons brandy (optional)

1. Preheat oven to 425°F.

2. Sprinkle duckling quarters with salt. Place on a rack in a shallow, open roasting pan. Prick each piece well with a fork.

3. Roast, uncovered and pricking often, 30 minutes. Remove from oven; reduce oven temperature to 375°F. Remove duckling and rack from pan.

4. Drain off all but 1 tablespoon fat from pan. Stir flour into fat in pan until smooth. Gradually stir in chicken broth and wine. Bring to boiling over direct heat; boil gently 1 minute. Add duckling, turning to coat with sauce.

5. Roast, uncovered and basting occasionally, 1 to 1¼ hours, or until fork-tender and golden.

6. Meanwhile, with vegetable parer, remove peel from oranges. Then remove white pulp from oranges. Cut peel into ⅛-inch-wide pieces. Cut oranges into ¼-inch-thick slices; halve each slice.

7. Place peel in medium saucepan. Cover with water; bring to boiling. Drain, remove and set aside.

8. In same saucepan, combine orange juice, sugar, and corn syrup; bring to boiling, stirring to dissolve sugar. Add orange peel; simmer, uncovered, 10 minutes. Stir in orange slices and brandy. Set aside.

9. Remove duckling to heated serving platter. Skim off all fat from roasting pan. Add orange mixture to roasting pan; bring to boiling, stirring to loosen browned bits. Pour over duckling.

Makes 4 servings.

Casserole of Duck and Beans

CASSOULET

2 packages (1-pound size) dried
  white Great Northern beans,
  or 2 pounds flageolets
8 cloves garlic
8 sprigs parsley
3 (3-inch) celery tops
8 whole cloves
6 cups sliced onion
4- to 5-pound ready-to-cook
  duckling
Salt
Pepper
1 medium onion, quartered

1 stalk celery, cut in half
2½-pound boneless smoked
  pork-shoulder butt
1 pound Polish sausage
8 slices bacon
2 cans (10½-ounce size)
  condensed beef broth
2 cans (8-ounce size) tomato
  sauce
2 teaspoons dried thyme leaves
4 bay leaves
2 cups dry white wine

1. In a 6-quart kettle, bring 3 quarts water to boiling. Add beans; return to boiling; boil 2 minutes. Remove from heat; let stand 1 hour. (Or soak beans in 3 quarts cold water overnight.)

2. On square of cheesecloth, place 4 cloves garlic, peeled, the parsley, celery tops, and cloves; tie cloth to form a bag. Add to beans, along with 2 cups sliced onion. Bring to boiling; skim surface. Reduce heat, and simmer, covered, 1½ hours, or until beans are just tender. Remove and discard cheesecloth bag.

3. Meanwhile, roast duckling: Preheat oven to 425°F. Remove and discard neck, liver, and giblets. Wash duck well inside and out; drain. Sprinkle inside and out with salt and pepper; place onion quarters and celery stalk in body cavity. Place duckling, breast side up, on rack in shallow roasting pan.

4. Roast, uncovered, 30 minutes; reduce oven temperature to 375°F; roast about 1½ hours longer, or until leg moves easily at joint.

5. Cool in pan until cool enough to handle. Remove from pan, reserving drippings. Cut meat from bones in large pieces; set aside; discard bones.

6. Meanwhile, place pork butt in large kettle; add water to cover; bring to boiling; reduce heat; simmer 1½ hours, or until tender when tested with a fork.

7. Slash sausage in several places. Cook in boiling water with pork butt during last 30 minutes.

8. Cut bacon in 1-inch pieces. Sauté in large skillet until crisp. Remove pieces; set aside.

9. Crush remaining garlic cloves; sauté in bacon drippings with remaining sliced onion until golden—about 5 minutes. Stir in the undiluted beef broth, tomato sauce, dried thyme leaves, bay leaves, and the reserved bacon bits; heat to boiling. Remove from heat.

10. Preheat oven to 350°F.

11. Cut 6 or 7 slices from pork butt; set aside. Cut the rest in 1-inch cubes.

12. Drain beans. Stir tomato mixture into beans; stir in wine, pieces of duck, and pork-butt cubes. Skim all fat from drippings from the duckling, and discard. Add drippings to bean mixture.

13. Turn into a shallow, 8-quart casserole. Place sausage on top; arrange slices of pork butt, overlapping, in center.

14. Bake, uncovered, 1½ hours, or until bubbling in center.

15. To serve: Remove sausage; slice in ¼-inch slices; arrange slices on top of beans.

Makes 12 to 15 servings.

Note: This is delicious prepared the day before, refrigerated, and reheated, covered, in 350°F oven until bubbling and hot.

Carmel Custard

Mousse au Chocolat

Breast of Chicken Parisienne

Bouillabaisse

Fruit Tartlets

Meats

The French take their time with meat. They consider our frequent consumption of hastily broiled unadorned beef to be slightly barbaric at worst and at best a sign of our lack of respect for meat. While plain broiled steak can certainly be a delight, there is no doubt that we Americans do eat it too often. And we would do well to learn to treat meat, and in particular beef, with some of the calm consideration that the French bring to it.

Most frequently, they braise meat, browning it in butter and then simmering it slowly with other ingredients designed to bring out its own best flavors, whether it be with red wine as in the famous Beef Bourguignon or with white wine and cloves as in Beef à la Mode. They combine it with herbs, with mushrooms, even with pastry, always seeking not to conceal the flavor of meat but how to enhance it best. Even when the French do serve steak or a rare piece of beef it is almost always accompanied by a sauce like a tangy mustard sauce, a red wine-based Bordelaise (page 71) or the king of French meat sauces, Béarnaise (page 72), or else it is rubbed or pricked with pepper and showered with wine or brandy as in Steak au Poivre.

Lamb is as popular as beef in France. And no wonder, for the French have a single secret with lamb that Americans have only just begun to listen in upon. They eat their lamb rare and pink. We tend to eat lamb well done, which makes the meat of this young creature rubbery in texture and coarse in flavor. Lamb eaten rare is a superb delicacy, no matter what the recipe, whether it be baked in a pastry crust or cooked with white beans in the traditional way of Brittany.

Veal and pork, too, are also popular in France and are cooked in a wide variety of ways. French veal is more delicate than American, for the calves are often kept on a milk diet that produces a whiter, more tender meat than does our American grass and grain diet for calves. When shopping for veal in the United States, look for light almost white meat to obtain the tastiest results.

Pepper Steak

STEAK AU POIVRE

3-pound boneless sirloin steak	1 tablespoon salad oil
2 tablespoons freshly cracked black pepper	½ cup dry white or red wine
2 tablespoons butter or margarine	2 tablespoons brandy
	1 teaspoon salt

1. Wipe steak with damp paper towels. Rub 1 tablespoon pepper into each side.

2. Slowly heat a large, heavy skillet until very hot. Add 1 tablespoon butter and the oil, stirring until butter is melted.

3. Add steak; over high heat, brown steak well on each side—about 2 minutes a side. Then reduce heat to medium, and cook 8 to 10 minutes a side for medium rare. Remove steak to a heated serving platter, and keep warm.

4. Add remaining butter, wine, brandy, and salt to skillet; simmer, stirring, 3 minutes. Pour over steak.

Makes 6 servings.

Steak with Mustard Sauce

STEAK À LA MOUTARDE

2 (1-pound size) club steaks	½ teaspoon salt
½ cup butter or margarine	⅛ teaspoon pepper
½ cup dry white wine	1 tablespoon Dijon mustard
1 beef-bouillon cube, dissolved in ½ cup boiling water	1 tablespoon dried tarragon leaves

1. Wipe steaks with damp paper towels; trim excess fat.

2. Slowly heat a large, heavy skillet. Add butter; heat. In hot butter, brown steaks, turning on each side.

3. Reduce heat; continue cooking steaks, turning, about 10 minutes in all, or until of desired doneness. Remove to heated platter; keep warm.

4. Add wine to skillet; bring to boiling, stirring to dissolve browned bits in pan. Continue boiling until almost evaporated.

5. Add beef bouillon, salt, and pepper. Continue boiling until reduced by half—about 5 minutes.

6. Meanwhile, spread steaks with mustard; sprinkle with tarragon.

7. Pour sauce in skillet over steaks. Serve at once.

Makes 4 servings.

Beef Slices in Wine

BOEUF AU VIN ROUGE

2-pound flank steak	1 can (8 ounce size)
(U. S. prime or choice)	tomato sauce
¼ cup butter or margarine	1 cup dry red wine
2 cloves garlic, crushed	½ pound fresh mushrooms,
¼ cup chopped parsley	thinly sliced
½ teaspoon salt	1 tablespoon flour
¼ teaspoon dried rosemary leaves	
¼ teaspoon dried basil leaves	1 package (8 ounce size) noodles
¼ teaspoon dried oregano leaves	2 tablespoons chopped parsley

1. Wipe steak with damp paper towels. With sharp knife, trim excess fat.

2. Cut steak crosswise into diagonal slices ¼ inch thick.

3. In hot butter in large Dutch oven, sauté slices, a few at a time, until browned on both sides. As slices brown, remove them from Dutch oven. Continue until all slices are browned. Remove from heat. Pour off drippings from pan.

4. Add garlic, ¼ cup parsley, the salt, rosemary, basil, oregano, tomato sauce, and wine. Put back meat.

5. Simmer, covered and stirring occasionally, about 1 hour, or until meat is tender.

6. Add mushrooms; simmer, covered, 5 minutes longer.

7. In small bowl, combine 2 tablespoons water and the flour; mix well. Stir into beef mixture; bring to boiling, stirring. Reduce heat; simmer 1 minute, or until mixture is thickened.

8. Meanwhile, cook noodles as package label directs; drain.

9. To serve: Spoon beef into center of deep serving dish; surround with noodles. Sprinkle with 2 tablespoons chopped parsley.

Makes 6 servings.

Tournedos with Béarnaise Sauce
TOURNEDOS, SAUCE BÉARNAISE

3 tablespoons butter or margarine	2 tablespoons butter or margarine, melted
6 (3-inch) white-bread rounds	Salt
	Pepper
6 slices filet of beef, 1 inch thick (3 pounds)	Béarnaise Sauce, page 72

1. In 3 tablespoons hot butter in large skillet, sauté bread rounds until lightly browned all over. Set aside.

2. Wipe the beef with damp paper towels. Arrange on greased broiler rack; brush with 1 tablespoon melted butter; sprinkle with ½ teaspoon salt and ⅛ teaspoon pepper.

3. Broil, 4 inches from heat, 5 minutes. Turn steaks; brush with remaining melted butter; sprinkle with ½ teaspoon salt and ⅛ teaspoon pepper. Broil 5 minutes longer, for medium rare.

4. To serve: Arrange meat on bread rounds on a heated platter. Garnish with watercress, if desired. Pass sauce.

Makes 6 servings.

Note: Serve Tournedos with Bordelaise Sauce (p. 71) instead of Béarnaise Sauce, if desired.

Beef Bourguignon
BOEUF BOURGUIGNON

Butter or margarine	2 tablespoons tomato paste
2½ pounds boneless beef chuck, cut into 1½-inch cubes	1½ cups Burgundy
3 tablespoons brandy	¾ cup dry sherry
½ pound small white onions, peeled (about 12)	¾ cup ruby port
½ pound small fresh mushrooms	1 can (10½ ounces) condensed beef bouillon, undiluted
2½ tablespoons potato flour	⅛ teaspoon pepper
2 to 2½ teaspoons meat-extract paste*	1 bay leaf

Do not use liquid meat extract.

1. Slowly heat a 4-quart Dutch oven with tight-fitting lid. Add 2 tablespoons butter; heat—do not burn.

2. In hot butter, over high heat, brown beef cubes well all over (about a fourth at a time—just enough to cover bottom of Dutch oven).

3. Lift out beef as it browns. Continue until all beef is browned, adding more butter as needed. Then return beef to Dutch oven.

4. In small saucepan, heat 2 tablespoons brandy just until vapor rises. Ignite, and pour over beef. As flame dies, remove beef cubes; set aside.

5. Add 2 tablespoons butter to Dutch oven; heat slightly. Add onions; cook over low heat, covered, until onions brown slightly. Then add mushrooms; cook, stirring, 3 minutes. Remove from heat.

6. Stir in flour, meat-extract paste, and tomato paste until well blended. Stir in Burgundy, sherry, port, and bouillon.

7. Preheat oven to 350°F.

8. Bring wine mixture just to boiling, stirring; remove from heat. Add beef, pepper, and bay leaf; mix well.

9. Bake, covered and stirring occasionally, 1½ hours, or until beef is tender, adding remaining brandy, little by little.

Makes 6 servings.

Note: This dish is better if made the day before, refrigerated, and reheated gently for serving. (If necessary, add a little more wine, to thin the sauce.)

Braised Beef

BOEUF À LA MODE

4-pound beef rump roast	Parsley sprig
2 tablespoons butter or margarine	¾ cup hot water
	3 whole cloves
2 cups dry white wine	12 white onions, peeled
1½ teaspoons salt	2 tablespoons brandy
¼ teaspoon pepper	6 medium carrots, pared and
½ bay leaf	quartered
½ teaspoon dried thyme leaves	¼ cup unsifted all-purpose flour
¼ teaspoon nutmeg	

1. Wipe beef with damp paper towels. Remove excess fat.

2. Slowly heat butter in large Dutch oven. Brown beef well on all sides—takes about 30 minutes.

3. Add wine, salt, pepper, bay leaf, thyme, nutmeg, parsley, and ½ cup hot water; bring just to boiling. Reduce heat; simmer, covered, 2½ hours.

4. Insert cloves in one onion. Add brandy, carrots, and all the onions. Simmer, covered, 1 hour longer, or just until beef is fork-tender. Discard onion with cloves.

5. To serve: Remove beef from cooking liquid to warm serving platter. With slotted utensil, lift vegetables from cooking liquid and surround beef; keep warm.

6. Combine ¼ cup water with the flour; mix to a smooth paste. Stir into liquid in Dutch oven; bring just to boiling, stirring until thickened. Pass gravy.

Makes 8 to 10 servings.

Lamb-Chop Casserole

CÔTES D'AGNEAU CHAMPVALLON

⅓ cup butter or margarine, melted	Salt
	Pepper
6 shouder lamb chops (about 3½ pounds)	1 cup canned chicken broth
2 cups finely chopped onion	2 parsley sprigs
1 clove garlic, crushed	4 whole cloves
	1 pound potatoes

1. Preheat oven to 350°F.

2. In half of hot butter in large skillet, brown chops, turning on both sides and adding more butter as needed—takes about 20 minutes.

3. As the chops brown, remove them to a 13-by-9-by-2-inch baking dish.

4. In drippings in skillet, sauté onion and garlic until tender—about 5 minutes.

5. Sprinkle onion-garlic mixture over chops; then sprinkle with 1 teaspoon salt and ¼ teaspoon pepper. Pour on chicken broth; add parsley sprigs and cloves.

6. Bake, covered, 30 minutes.

7. Meanwhile, pare potatoes, and thinly slice. Arrange over top of chops; sprinkle with 1 teaspoon salt and ¼ teaspoon pepper.

8. Bake, covered, 30 minutes, or until potatoes are tender. Bake, uncovered, 30 minutes longer, or until golden.

Makes 6 servings.

Leg of Lamb in Pastry
GIGOT D'AGNEAU EN CROÛTE

3 or 4 lamb kidneys
(½ pound)
3 tablespoons butter or
margarine
1 tablespoon Madeira
¼ pound fresh mushrooms,
chopped
¾ teaspoon salt
½ teaspoon dried rosemary
leaves
¼ teaspoon dried thyme leaves
¼ teaspoon dried tarragon
leaves

4- to 4½-pound leg-of-lamb roast,
boned but not tied
Soft butter or margarine

1 package piecrust mix
1 egg yolk

2 tablespoons butter or
margarine
2 tablespoons flour
3 tablespoons Madeira
1½ tablespoons red-currant jelly

1. Remove fat and white veins from kidneys; wash, and dry with paper towels. Finely dice kidneys.

2. In 3 tablespoons hot butter in skillet, sauté kidney until golden. Stir in 1 tablespoon wine, the mushrooms, salt, rosemary, thyme, and tarragon. Remove from heat.

3. Preheat oven to 425°F.

4. Wipe lamb with damp paper towels; trim off most of fat. Fill with kidney mixture. Form into compact roast; secure with skewers. Rub with soft butter—about 2 tablespoons. Place on rack in shallow roasting pan. Insert meat thermometer into thickest part of meat, not in kidney mixture.

5. Roast, uncovered, 60 minutes, or until thermometer registers 150°F.

6. Meanwhile, make pastry from piecrust mix, following label directions. On lightly floured surface, roll pastry into 15-by-12-inch oval.

7. Remove roast from oven. Place roast in shallow baking pan without a rack. Remove thermometer and skewers. Reserve drippings in pan.

8. Lay pastry over roast, pressing against meat and tucking underneath, to cover roast completely. Beat egg yolk with 1 teaspoon water; brush over pastry.

9. Bake in 450°F oven 15 to 20 minutes, or until pastry is golden.

10. Meanwhile, add 1 cup water to reserved drippings in roasting pan; heat, stirring to loosen browned bits. Strain into 2-cup measure; skim off fat. There should be about 1 cup drippings remaining.

11. Melt butter in small saucepan. Stir in flour, and cook, stirring con-

stantly, until slightly golden. Gradually add strained drippings; cook over medium heat, stirring constantly, until thickened; boil gently 1 minute. Stir in wine and jelly. Keep warm. Serve with roast.

Makes 8 servings.

Roast Loin of Pork Boulanger

RÔTI DE PORC BOULANGER

5-pounds loin of pork	1 can (10½ ounces) condensed
1 teaspoon salt	chicken broth, undiluted
½ teaspoon rubbed sage	1 tablespoon chopped parsley
Pepper	2 teaspoons seasoned salt
8 potatoes, pared and halved	2 tablespoons flour
(3 pounds)	2 tablespoons water
2 cups sliced onion	

1. Preheat oven to 375°F.

2. Wipe pork with damp paper towels. Rub with salt, sage, and ¼ teaspoon pepper. Place, fat side up, in shallow, open roasting pan. Insert meat thermometer into center of meaty part of pork; it should not rest on bone.

3. Roast, uncovered, 1½ hours. Remove from oven. Reduce oven temperature to 350°F.

4. Remove pork from roasting pan; discard all drippings. In roasting pan combine potatoes, onion, chicken broth, parsley, seasoned salt, and ¼ teaspoon pepper; toss gently to blend. Top with pork. Cover pan tightly with lid or foil.

5. Roast, covered, 1 to 1¼ hours, or until thermometer registers 185°F.

6. Remove pork to deep serving dish. Spoon vegetables around meat and sprinkle potatoes with more chopped parsley, if desired. (If you prefer the potatoes browned, run under broiler for about 5 minutes before placing around the pork.)

7. Combine flour and 2 tablespoons water, stirring to make a smooth paste. Stir into juices in roasting pan (juices should measure 2 cups). Bring to boiling; reduce heat, and simmer 3 minutes.

Makes 6 to 8 servings.

Veal Ragout Parisienne

RAGOÛT DE VEAU À LA PARISIENNE

1 tablespoon butter or
  margarine
2 pound boned veal shoulder,
  cut in 1-inch cubes
1½ cups boiling water
1 envelope (0.7 ounce)
  onion-salad-dressing mix
¾ teaspoon salt
½ teaspoon dried
  marjoram leaves

1½ cups pared and cut-up
  carrot (1-inch pieces)
1 cup sliced celery
2 medium yellow summer
  squash, sliced (about 3 cups)
1 package (10 ounces)
  frozen peas
1 tablespoon flour
2 tablespoons water

1. In hot butter in 4-quart Dutch oven, brown veal well on all sides.

2. Gradually stir in boiling water, salad-dressing mix, salt, and marjoram. Bring to boiling; reduce heat, and simmer, covered, ½ hour.

3. Add carrot to meat mixture; simmer, covered, about ½ hour.

4. Add celery and yellow squash, pressing them into the liquid; cook 10 minutes. Add peas; cook 15 minutes, or until all vegetables are tender.

5. Remove meat and vegetables to heated serving dish; keep warm.

6. Mix flour with 2 tablespoons water until smooth. Stir into liquid in Dutch oven; bring to boiling, and boil 1 minute, or until slightly thick. Spoon over meat and vegetables.

Makes 6 servings.

Roast Leg of Veal in White Wine

GIGOT DE VEAU AU VIN BLANC

4 slices bacon
7-pound leg of veal,*
  boned but not tied
Salt
Pepper
½ teaspoon dried rosemary
  leaves

2 large cloves garlic,
  finely chopped
⅓ cup chopped parsley
½ cup white wine
2 tablespoons butter or
  margarine
2 tablespoons flour

1. Cut bacon in ½-inch pieces. Fry until crisp; drain. Set bacon drippings aside to cool.

2. Preheat oven to 350°F. Wipe veal with damp paper towels. On

Veal weighs 9 pounds before boning.

waxed paper, combine 1 teaspoon salt, ½ teaspoon pepper, and the rosemary.

3. Spread veal flat, skin side down on work surface. Cut four slits, about 1½ inches deep, in thickest part of meat.

4. Rub half of salt mixture over top of veal and into slits; then spread veal evenly with bacon drippings, garlic, and parsley; sprinkle with bacon bits. Carefully bring ends together, and tie with twine securely into a well-shaped roll.

5. Rub remaining salt mixture over veal roll. Place on rack in shallow, open roasting pan. Insert meat thermometer into the thickest part of veal.

6. Roast, uncovered, 30 minutes. Pour wine over veal. Roast, basting frequently with pan drippings, 2 to 2½ hours longer, or until meat thermometer registers 170°F. Add ½ cup water to pan if necessary. Remove veal to serving platter.

7. Pour drippings into a 2-cup measure. Skim off excess fat, and discard. Add water to drippings to measure 1½ cups. Return to roasting pan; bring to boiling, stirring to dissolve all browned bits in pan. Boil 1 minute; remove from heat, and strain if desired.

8. Melt butter in medium saucepan; remove from heat. Stir in flour until smooth; cook 3 minutes. Remove from heat. Gradually stir in hot liquid; bring to boiling. Reduce heat, and simmer 3 to 5 minutes. Season with salt and pepper to taste. Serve with veal.

Makes 12 to 14 servings.

Veal Chops with Mushrooms

CÔTES DE VEAU AUX CHAMPIGNONS

4 veal loin chops, 1¼ inches thick (about 2½ pounds)	1 teaspoon salt
⅓ cup butter or margarine	⅛ teaspoon pepper
½ pound fresh mushrooms, sliced; or 1 can (6 ounces) sliced mushrooms, drained	1 can (10½ ounces) condensed beef bouillon, undiluted
2 tablespoons lemon juice	⅔ cup dry white wine
½ cup sliced onion	1 teaspoon chopped fresh tarragon leaves
½ clove garlic, crushed	1 teaspoon liquid gravy seasoning
¼ cup flour	½ teaspoon dry chives
	⅛ teaspoon pepper

1. Wipe chops with damp paper towels. Trim excess fat. Roll up ends of chops, and secure with wooden picks.

2. In hot butter in Dutch oven or deep skillet, brown chops on both sides. Remove chops, and set aside.

3. Sprinkle mushrooms with lemon juice. Add with onion and garlic to drippings in Dutch oven; sauté until golden—about 5 minutes. Remove from heat. With slotted spoon, remove sautéed vegetables, and set aside with chops.

4. Stir flour, salt, and pepper into pan drippings until well blended. Gradually stir in bouillon and wine. Add tarragon, gravy seasoning, chives, and pepper.

5. Bring to boiling, stirring occasionally. Add chops and sautéed vegetables; reduce heat, and simmer, covered, 30 minutes, or until chops are tender.

6. To serve: Remove chops to heated serving platter, and remove picks. Spoon vegetables and some of gravy over chops. Pass rest of gravy.

Makes 4 servings.

Sauces

Sauces are an integral part of French cooking. Superb sauces are traditional in haute cuisine and a chef usually spends several years apprenticeship just in perfecting his sauces. But excellent sauces are not limited to the food found in the great restaurants; every French housewife makes delicious sauces as a matter of course, for even simple, everyday cooking is treated as an art. The average French person almost certainly eats more delicious food than the rest of the world, and one of the reasons is the sauces that embellish his food—they are both good in themselves and complement whatever they accompany.

A sauce is the touch that lifts a dish out of the ordinary; a sauce can transform an inexpensive cut of meat, turn leftovers into gourmet fare, and stretch expensive ingredients so that even the homemaker with a tight budget can occasionally indulge in dishes made with lobster, filet mignon, or truffles.

The secret of French sauces is good fresh ingredients, discreet seasoning by cooks with a subtle sense of taste, and careful attention to the cooking method. The French prefer to cook with butter for it gives the best flavor. The sauces usually begin with a good deal of liquid—wine, meat, fish, or vegetable stock (water vegetables were cooked in), which is then simmered down, intensifying all the flavors.

Red Wine and Shallot Sauce

SAUCE BORDELAISE

This is a classic sauce for beef and is particularly good with panbroiled steak. In France, stock made with beef bones instead of bouillon would be used, and then the marrow from the bones would be diced and added to the sauce.

¼ cup butter or margarine	3 tablespoons flour
2 shallots, finely chopped	½ teaspoon meat-extract paste*
2 cloves garlic, finely chopped	1 can (10½ ounces) condensed
2 slices onion	beef bouillon, undiluted
2 slices carrot	1 cup Burgundy
2 sprigs parsley	2 tablespoons finely chopped
10 whole black peppers	parsley
2 whole cloves	¼ teaspoon salt
2 bay leaves	⅛ teaspoon pepper

1. In hot butter in medium skillet, sauté shallots, garlic, onion, carrot, parsley, peppers, cloves, and bay leaves until onion is golden—about 3 minutes. Remove from heat.

2. Stir in flour until well blended; cook over very low heat, stirring, until flour is lightly browned—about 5 minutes. Remove from heat.

3. Stir in meat-extract paste, bouillon, and ¾ cup Burgundy; over medium heat, bring just to boiling, stirring constantly. Reduce heat; simmer, uncovered and stirring occasionally, 10 minutes.

4. Strain sauce, discarding vegetables, and spices. Return sauce to skillet. Add parsley, salt, pepper, rest of wine; reheat gently—do not boil.

5. Taste; add more meat-extract paste, if desired.

Makes 2 cups. Serve with beef.

Hollandaise Sauce

SAUCE HOLLANDAISE

This rich and delicious sauce makes vegetables such as asparagus, green beans, broccoli, and cauliflower worthy of being served as a separate course. It is also excellent with broiled or poached fish and poached eggs.

While Hollandaise is easy to make successfully, remember that the secret is to stir the sauce constantly, never letting the water boil in the

*Do not use liquid meat extract.

bottom of the double boiler, and to add the butter slowly, making sure each addition is thoroughly beaten into the sauce before adding more.

If the sauce should separate or curdle, it can be brought back every time by this method: Beat 1 teaspoon each of lemon juice and sauce in a warm bowl with a wire whisk until creamy, then slowly beat in the curdled sauce, beating after each addition until creamy.

Hollandaise is always served warm, never hot. Overheating the sauce after it is made is often the reason for its separating.

2 egg yolks	1½ tablespoons lemon juice
¼ cup butter or margarine, melted	¼ teaspoon salt
¼ cup boiling water	Dash cayenne

1. In top of double boiler, with wire whisk or fork, slightly beat egg yolks.

2. Slowly stir in butter. Gradually add water, beating constantly.

3. Cook, stirring, over hot water (hot water in double-boiler base should not touch pan above), just until thickened.

4. Remove double-boiler top from hot water. Gradually beat lemon juice, salt, and cayenne into sauce.

5. Cover, and keep hot over warm water until serving.

Makes about ⅔ cup.

Hollandaise with Whipped Cream

SAUCE MOUSSELINE

Hollandaise Sauce, page 71	¼ cup heavy cream, whipped

1. Prepare Hollandaise Sauce as recipe directs.
2. Just before serving, fold in whipped cream.

Makes about 1 cup.

Lemon-butter Sauce with Tarragon

SAUCE BÉARNAISE

Serve this sauce with steaks, broiled or poached fish, chicken, and eggs. Since Béarnaise is made like Hollandaise, see the beginning of instructions to the recipe for Hollandaise Sauce (page 71).

¼ cup tarragon vinegar
¼ cup dry white wine
2 tablespoons finely chopped
   fresh tarragon, or 2 teaspoons
   dried tarragon leaves

1 tablespoon finely chopped
   shallot
3 egg yolks
½ cup butter or margarine

1. In small saucepan, combine vinegar, wine, 1 tablespoon tarragon, and the shallot; bring just to boiling over medium heat. Reduce heat and simmer, uncovered, until the liquid is reduced to ¼ cup—will take 8 to 10 minutes.

2. Strain mixture into top of double boiler. With wire whisk or rotary beater, beat in egg yolks. Cook over hot, not boiling, water, beating constantly, until mixture begins to thicken.

3. Beat in butter, 1 tablespoon at a time, beating well after each addition, to melt butter. Stir remaining chopped tarragon into sauce. Serve at once, with steak, or keep warm until serving time. (Add just enough cold water to hot water in bottom of double boiler to make it lukewarm. Set double boiler top with sauce over water, and set aside, covered.)

Makes about 1 cup.

White Sauce with Herbs and Lemon
SAUCE MAÎTRE D'HÔTEL

¼ cup butter or margarine
¼ cup finely chopped onion
¼ cup unsifted all-purpose flour
1 teaspoon salt
Dash cayenne
2 cups milk

⅓ cup lemon juice
1½ tablespoons chopped parsley
1½ tablespoons chopped fresh
   tarragon leaves, or 1½ teaspoons
   dried tarragon leaves
2 egg yolks, beaten

1. In hot butter in medium saucepan, sauté onion 3 minutes. Remove from heat. Stir in flour, salt, and cayenne. Gradually stir in milk.

2. Bring to boiling; reduce heat, and simmer 5 minutes, stirring occasionally.

3. Stir in lemon juice, parsley, and tarragon.

4. Stir some of hot mixture into egg yolks, combining well. Return to saucepan; heat slightly.

Makes about 2½ cups.

Cheese Sauce

SAUCE MORNAY

2 tablespoons butter or margarine	¼ cup heavy cream
2 tablespoons flour	1 cup milk
½ teaspoon salt	¼ cup grated natural Swiss cheese

1. Melt butter in small saucepan; remove from heat. Stir in flour and salt. Gradually stir in cream and milk.
2. Bring to boiling, stirring; reduce heat, and simmer the mixture for 1 minute.
3. Add cheese; stir, over low heat, just until cheese is melted.
Makes 1⅓ cups.

Mushroom Sauce

SAUCE AUX CHAMPIGNONS

1 can (10½ ounces) condensed cream-of-mushroom soup, undiluted	½ cup light cream
	1 teaspoon instant coffee
	2 teaspoons chopped pimiento

1. In medium saucepan, combine mushroom soup with rest of ingredients; mix well.
2. Over low heat, simmer, stirring occasionally, until hot—about 10 minutes.
Makes about 1½ cups.

Orange Sauce

SAUCE ORANGE

This is the sauce for Orange-glazed Roast Duckling, but it is also delicious on other roast poultry.

3 large oranges	3 tablespoons brandy
3 tablespoons butter or margarine	¾ teaspoon minced garlic
Liver from duckling	2 tablespoons flour
	2 tablespoons catsup

Filets de Sole Bonne Femme

Coquilles St.-Jacques

Eggs in Aspic

Beef Bourguignon

1½ teaspoons meat-extract paste*   ⅓ cup Burgundy
⅛ teaspoon pepper   ¼ cup orange marmalade
1 can (10½ ounces) condensed
   chicken broth, undiluted

1. Grate peel from 1 orange, and reserve 2 tablespoons. Holding oranges over bowl to catch juice, peel with sharp knife; remove sections; set aside. Reserve ¼ cup orange juice.

2. In 2 tablespoons hot butter in medium skillet, brown duckling liver well. Remove pan from heat.

3. Heat brandy slightly in small saucepan. Ignite; slowly pour over liver. When flames subside, remove liver; set aside.

4. Add remaining butter, reserved grated peel, and garlic to skillet; sauté 3 minutes. Remove from heat. Stir in flour, catsup, meat-extract paste, and pepper until well blended. Gradually stir in chicken broth, Burgundy, marmalade, and reserved orange juice.

5. Bring to boiling, stirring constantly. Reduce heat, and simmer, stirring occasionally, 15 minutes.

6. Meanwhile, chop liver. Add to sauce along with orange sections. Heat gently.

Makes 2 cups.

White Wine Sauce

SAUCE AU VIN BLANC

¼ pound mushrooms   1 cup strained cooking liquid
2 tablespoons butter or   from poaching fish
   margarine   ¼ cup dry white wine
2 tablespoons flour   ½ cup heavy cream
½ teaspoon salt   1 egg yolk, slightly beaten

1. Wash mushrooms; slice thickly down through stem.

2. Melt butter in medium saucepan. Add mushrooms, and sauté 5 minutes. Remove from heat. Stir in flour and salt, to make a smooth mixture.

3. Gradually stir in cooking liquid from fish, the wine, and cream.

4. Bring just to boiling, stirring. Reduce heat; simmer 5 minutes.

5. Stir a little of hot mixture into egg yolk, mixing well. Pour back into saucepan; mix well. Cook, stirring, a few minutes longer.

Makes 1¾ cups.

Do not use liquid meat extract.

Lobster Sauce

SAUCE HOMARD

Serve this sauce with poached fish or quenelles.

Salt	1½ tablespoons flour
2 (6-ounce size)	Dash paprika
frozen lobster tails	1 cup light cream
3 tablespoons butter or	2 egg yolks, slightly beaten
margarine	3 tablespoons dry sherry

1. In medium saucepan, bring 4 cups water with ½ teaspoon salt to boiling. Add lobster tails; boil gently 5 minutes. Drain.

2. Remove lobster meat from shells. Cut meat into pieces—there should be about 1¼ cups. Set aside.

3. Melt butter in medium saucepan. Remove from heat. Stir in flour, ½ teaspoon salt, and the paprika. Gradually stir in cream.

4. Bring to boiling over medium heat, stirring until mixture thickens.

5. Stir a little hot mixture into egg yolks; return to saucepan.

6. Add sherry and lobster; bring just to boiling. Keep warm.
Makes 2 cups.

Parsley Butter

BEURRE MAITRE D'HOTEL

½ cup soft butter	⅛ teaspoon pepper
2 tablespoons lemon juice	2½ tablespoons finely chopped
½ teaspoon salt	parsley

1. In small bowl, with wooden spoon, or portable electric mixer at medium speed, beat butter until light.

2. Beat in rest of ingredients. Chill.

3. Turn out on waxed paper. Shape into a cylinder, 1 to 1½ inches in diameter. Wrap in waxed paper.

4. Refrigerate until well chilled. To serve, slice crosswise into ½-inch-thick pats.

5. To serve hot: Melt butter in small skillet; add rest of ingredients.
Makes 8 servings.

Garlic Butter

BEURRE D'AIL

Make Parsley Butter, page 76, substituting ¼ teaspoon crushed garlic for the lemon juice.

Wine Butter

BEURRE AU VIN

Make Parsley Butter, page 76, substituting ⅓ cup dry white wine for the lemon juice.

Butter Sauce

SAUCE AU BEURRE

Cooking liquid from asparagus or other vegetable	2 teaspoons flour
6 tablespoons butter or margarine	2 teaspoons lemon juice
	Chopped parsley

1. Measure asparagus liquid. Return to skillet; bring to boiling. Reduce to ⅔ cup.

2. Melt butter in same skillet. Stir in flour until smooth. Gradually add vegetable liquid and lemon juice; bring to boiling, stirring constantly. Reduce heat; simmer 3 minutes. Pour over asparagus or other vegetable; sprinkle with parsley, and serve.

Makes about ⅔ cup.

Red Wine Butter Sauce

BEURRE MARCHAND DE VINS

This is best served at room temperature with steak or other broiled meat.

1 tablespoon minced shallot	2 teaspoons chopped parsley
1 cup dry red wine	Salt
½ cup soft butter or margarine	Pepper

1. Cook shallot in wine in small saucepan until liquid is reduced to ¼ cup. Remove the saucepan from heat; cool.

2. With electric mixer, cream butter with parsley. Gradually beat in wine-shallot mixture. Season to taste with salt and pepper.

Makes about ¾ cup.

Blender Mayonnaise
MAYONNAISE

Homemade mayonnaise is so superior to the commercial product that it is always worth making. The electric blender has simplified and quickened mayonnaise making and the following recipe is a never-fail one. Blender mayonnaise will keep for a week or more; it can be kept even longer if a tablespoon of boiling water is beaten in gradually after blending.

1 cup corn oil	⅛ teaspoon cayenne pepper
1 egg	2 tablespoons lemon juice, or
1 teaspoon salt	1 tablespoon lemon and
½ teaspoon dry mustard	1 tablespoon mild vinegar

1. Chill blender container and oil.

2. Break egg into blender container. Add salt, mustard, cayenne, lemon juice and/or vinegar, and ¼ cup oil.

3. Turn blender to low and immediately add remaining oil. Blend until mayonnaise is thick. It may be necessary to push mayonnaise toward center with rubber spatula.

Makes 1¼ cups.

French Dressing
SAUCE VINAIGRETTE

Vinaigrette is good poured over any cold green vegetable and goes particularly well with artichokes, asparagus, and green beans. It may be used as a salad dressing or with cold poached fish or julienne strips of cold roast beef.

1 cup olive or salad oil	2 tablespoons chopped chives
⅓ cup red-wine vinegar	1 teaspoon salt
2 tablespoons chopped capers	⅛ teaspoon pepper

1. Combine all ingredients in jar with tight-fitting lid. Shake well.

2. Refrigerate until ready to use. Shake again just before pouring over asparagus.

Makes 1½ cups.

Vegetables
& Green Salads

VEGETABLES
Légumes

Delicious vegetables are one of the many pleasures of the French table. They are almost always fresh, very rarely frozen or canned, and are eaten in season when they are at their peak. Tiny, young peas, petits pois, pencil-slender asparagus spears, or crisp little green beans are served nearly every day when they are plentiful. Then they are replaced by artichokes, carrots, cabbage, or whatever else the successive months offer. In this way the French do not have the daily variety of vegetables Americans are accustomed to; instead they have the pleasure of eating a vegetable when it is at its best and most flavorful.

Vegetables are so well thought of in France that they are usually served as a separate course after the entrée or meat course. Cooked to perfection, sometimes sauced, in combinations or alone, they deserve the attention they receive as a course in themselves. The vegetables that are served by themselves are most often artichokes, asparagus, cauliflower, endive, leeks (called the "asparagus of the poor"), mushrooms, and potato dishes like Pommes de Terre Anna. Certain vegetables classically accompany meats: Red cabbage is eaten with duck in the fall and winter, in summer, peas are served with duck; turnips are served with lamb or duck; peas and little white onions go with spring lamb; morilles, a mushroom from Alsace-Lorraine, flavors fish dishes; sauerkraut goes with game and smoked meats; Pommes de Terre Frites are traditional with rare steak.

The French also eat a number of vegetables that are not common in America: celery-like cardoons; celery root or céleri-rave; oyster plant or salsifis; and sorrel, which is used to flavor cream soups. They are particularly fond of wild mushrooms, cèpes, girolles, mousserons, and morilles. Lettuces, endive, chicory, and cucumbers are not only used in salads but are also braised in a little broth and served hot.

The method of cooking that brings out the most flavor in green vegetables is to blanch them in a large pot of rapidly boiling water until they are just tender but still crisp. The asparagus, green beans, or other vegetables are then plunged into cold water to stop the cooking process. They are drained and dried on paper towels. Just before serving, they are sautéed in a pan with butter or oil, flavored with a touch of fresh garlic or herbs, until heated through. Vegetables prepared like this can be cooked ahead, then the sautéing can be done just before serving. The other favorite French method of cooking vegetables is to braise them in a little broth or stock in a tightly covered pot. None of the flavor or vitamins is lost this way and the vegetables are sauced with the liquid they are cooked in. Mushrooms, cabbages, white onions, chestnuts—as well as most of the lettuces—benefit from this method of cooking.

Artichokes

ARTICHAUTS AU NATUREL

Artichokes cooked this way may be served with Hollandaise Sauce or melted butter flavored with lemon juice. They can also be chilled and served with a mayonnaise-based sauce or vinaigrette dressing.

¼ cup salad or olive oil	1 teaspoon salt
2 tablespoons lemon juice	Dash pepper
2 small bay leaves	4 large artichokes
1 clove garlic, split	(about 3 pounds)

1. In large kettle, boil 6 quarts water with oil, lemon juice, bay leaves, garlic, salt, and pepper.

2. Trim stalks from base and cut a 1-inch slice from top of each artichoke. Remove discolored leaves; snip off spike ends of leaves.

3. Wash artichokes in cold water; drain. Tie each with twine to hold leaves in place.

4. Add to boiling water. Reduce heat; simmer, covered, 30 minutes, or until base feels soft.

5. Drain artichokes well; remove twine.

Makes 4 servings.

Asparagus with Hollandaise Sauce

ASPERGES, SAUCE HOLLANDAISE

2 to 2½ pounds asparagus	¼ cup butter or
Boiling water	margarine, melted
½ teaspoon salt	Hollandaise Sauce, page 71

1. Break or cut off tough ends of asparagus. Wash asparagus well under cold running water. (If asparagus is sandy, scrub with brush. With a vegetable parer, scrape the skin and scales from just lower part of stalks.)

2. Bunch stalks together; tie with string, or use a rubber band. Place upright in deep saucepan. Add boiling water (about 2 inches deep) and the salt.

3. Then return to boiling, and cook, covered, 15 to 20 minutes. Pierce lower part of stalks with fork, to see if they are tender. Be sure not to overcook.

4. Drain asparagus well, being careful not to break stalks. Arrange in heated vegetable dish; pour butter over all. Serve with Hollandaise Sauce. (Or, if desired, omit hollandaise, and serve with lemon wedges.)

Makes 4 to 6 servings.

Green Beans Provençal

HARICOTS VERTS À LA PROVENÇALE

1 pound fresh green beans	1 teaspoon salt
1 medium tomato, peeled	Dash pepper
and chopped	½ teaspoon dried basil leaves
½ cup chopped green onion	2 tablespoons butter

1. Wash beans; drain. Trim ends; cut on the diagonal into 1-inch pieces.

2. Combine all ingredients in medium skillet. Cook, covered, over low heat, stirring occasionally, 10 to 15 minutes, or until beans are tender.

Makes 4 servings.

Brussels Sprouts with Chestnut Sauce

CHOUX DE BRUXELLES AUX MARRONS

1 pound brussels sprouts	½ pound chestnuts, roasted and
1 teaspoon salt	peeled; or 1 can (11 ounces)
	chestnuts, drained
	⅓ cup butter or margarine

1. Cut off stem ends of brussels sprouts. Soak sprouts in cold water 15 minutes; drain.

2. Place in medium saucepan with 3 cups water and the salt; bring to boiling. Lower heat, and simmer, uncovered, 10 minutes, or until tender. Drain.

3. Quarter chestnuts. Sauté in hot butter in saucepan 5 minutes. Toss with drained brussels sprouts.

Makes 6 servings.

Note: To roast chestnuts: First make a slit in each shell with a sharp knife. Bake at 500°F for 15 minutes. Remove shells and skin.

Carrots Vichy

CAROTTES VICHY

1 pound carrots	1 teaspoon sugar
2 tablespoons butter or	⅛ teaspoon salt
margarine	Chopped parsley

1. Pare carrots; slice paper-thin. Place in medium saucepan with ¼ cup water, the butter, sugar, and salt.

2. Cook over low heat, tightly covered, 20 minutes, or until carrots are tender and all liquid has evaporated. Garnish with parsley.

Makes 3 servings.

Mushrooms under Bell

CHAMPIGNONS SOUS CLOCHE

6 tablespoons soft butter	Dash pepper
or margarine	4 slices French bread,
1 tablespoon chopped parsley	½ inch thick, toasted
2 teaspoons lemon juice	1¼ pounds fresh mushrooms,
½ teaspoon salt	stems trimmed to ½ inch
¼ teaspoon dried chervil	½ cup heavy cream
leaves	2 tablespoons dry sherry

1. Preheat oven to 375°F. In a small bowl, beat butter with chopped parsley, lemon juice, salt, chervil leaves, and pepper. Use half of the mixture to spread on one side of toast slices. Place slices, buttered side up, in individual casseroles or ramekins.

2. Spread the mushrooms with remaining butter mixture. Mound mushrooms over toast, and drizzle with heavy cream. Cover with an ovenproof-glass "bell" or a cover.

3. Bake 20 minutes, or until mushrooms are just tender. Sprinkle each serving with sherry. Serve at once.

Makes 4 servings.

Glazed Onions and Turnips
OIGNONS ET NAVETS GLACÉS

20 small white onions, peeled	2 tablespoons butter or
4 white turnips, pared	margarine
and quartered	2 teaspoons sugar

1. Cook onions and turnips separately in 1-inch boiling salted water just until tender—15 to 25 minutes for onions, about 10 minutes for turnips. Drain each well.

2. Heat 1 tablespoon butter in large skillet; add onions, and sprinkle with 1 teaspoon sugar. Cook over medium heat, shaking pan often, until onions are golden and glazed—about 5 minutes. Turn into bowl, and keep warm.

3. Heat remaining butter in same skillet. Add turnips, and sprinkle with 1 teaspoon sugar. Cook until golden and glazed.

Makes 4 servings.

French-style Green Peas
PETITS POIS À LA FRANÇAISE

4 large lettuce leaves	½ teaspoon salt
3 pounds fresh young peas*	Dash pepper
1 teaspoon sugar	2 tablespoons butter

1. Line medium-sized, heavy skillet, with tight-fitting cover, with 3 lettuce leaves. Shell peas and add. Sprinkle with sugar, salt, pepper. Dot with butter; top with last lettuce leaf.

Note: Or use 1 package (10 ounce) frozen tiny peas. Cook 8 minutes, as directed above. Spread peas with a fork; cook 8 minutes longer, or until peas are tender. Makes 3 servings.

2. Cook over medium heat, tightly covered, 10 to 15 minutes, or until tender.

Makes 4 servings.

French-fried Potatoes

POMMES DE TERRE FRITES

Salad oil   3 large potatoes (about 2 pounds)

1. Fill large skillet or deep-fat fryer one-third full with salad oil. Slowly heat to 375°F on deep-frying thermometer.

2. Meanwhile, pare potatoes; cut lengthwise into quarters, then into slender sticks.

3. Fry potatoes, a single layer at a time, in hot oil about 10 minutes, or until golden brown and tender. Drain on paper towels. Keep warm.

Makes 4 servings.

Potatoes Anna

POMMES DE TERRE ANNA

½ cup soft butter or   1 teaspoon salt
  margarine   ⅛ teaspoon pepper
2 pounds Idaho potatoes,
  pared and thinly sliced
  (about 5 cups)

1. Preheat oven to 425°F. With 3 tablespoons butter, grease an 8-inch skillet with heat-resistant handle and tight-fitting cover.

2. Gently toss potatoes with salt and pepper. Layer a third of potato slices, circular fashion, around bottom and side of skillet. Dot with butter. Repeat twice.

3. Over high heat, cook potatoes 3 minutes. Then bake, covered, 30 minutes. (Place sheet of foil under skillet to catch any runover.) Remove cover; bake 5 minutes longer. Let stand 5 minutes; invert on platter.

Makes 6 servings.

Vegetable Casserole

RATATOUILLE

2 medium green peppers   1 medium eggplant
2 medium zucchini   (about 1 pound)

½ cup salad or olive oil
1 cup thinly sliced onion
2 cloves garlic, crushed
1½ teaspoons salt

4 medium tomatoes, peeled
and cut into wedges
2 tablespoons chopped parsley

1. Wash peppers; halve. Remove ribs and seeds. Cut lengthwise into ¼-inch-thick slices.

2. Scrub zucchini; cut crosswise into ½-inch-thick slices.

3. Wash eggplant; do not peel. Cut lengthwise into quarters; then cut crosswise into ¼-inch slices.

4. In ¼ cup hot oil in large skillet, sauté green-pepper slices, onion, and garlic about 5 minutes. With slotted spoon, remove to medium bowl.

5. Add 2 tablespoons oil to skillet. In hot oil, sauté zucchini, turning frequently, until tender—about 10 minutes. With slotted utensil, remove from skillet to a large bowl.

6. Add remaining 2 tablespoons oil to skillet. In hot oil, sauté eggplant, turning occasionally, until tender—about 5 minutes.

7. Remove eggplant from skillet with slotted utensil. Add to zucchini; toss lightly.

8. Return vegetables to same skillet in this order: Spoon half of green pepper mixture into skillet. Sprinkle with ¼ teaspoon salt and dash pepper. Top with half of zucchini-eggplant mixture; sprinkle with ¼ teaspoon salt and dash pepper.

9. Layer half of tomato wedges on top. Sprinkle with ¼ teaspoon salt and 1 tablespoon parsley.

10. Repeat with remaining pepper mixture, zucchini-eggplant mixture, tomatoes, salt, pepper, and parsley.

11. Simmer mixture, covered and over low heat, 2 minutes, basting occasionally with pan juices.

12. Remove cover; cook 5 minutes longer, basting occasionally, until liquid is evaporated.

13. Serve hot or very well chilled. Especially good with lamb.
Makes 8 to 10 servings.

Tomatoes Provençale

TOMATES À LA PROVENÇALE

4 large tomatoes (2 pounds)
3 tablespoons olive oil
½ teaspoon salt
Pepper

1 medium clove garlic, crushed
1 tablespoon chopped parsley
2 tablespoons coarse white
bread crumbs

1. Halve tomatoes crosswise, and remove seeds.

2. In hot oil in skillet, sauté tomatoes, cut side down, about 3 minutes. Turn; sprinkle with salt and dash of pepper; sauté 3 minutes.

3. Add garlic to skillet, and sauté 2 minutes longer, or just until tomatoes are tender. Remove tomatoes to heated serving dish; sprinkle with parsley.

4. Add bread crumbs to skillet, and cook over high heat until golden. Drain on paper towels; then sprinkle over tomatoes.

Makes 8 servings.

GREEN SALADS

Salades Simples

The main course, whether it is a light one—an omelet, cheese soufflé, or potatoes cooked with cheese and cream—or a stalwart roast or stew, is often followed by a simple green salad. The salad is composed of one or more greens—Boston or Bibb lettuce, romaine, chicory, Belgian endive, escarole, or watercress. In the spring, tender wild greens like dandelions are often added to the salad bowl.

The dressing is invariably a simple one of olive oil, wine vinegar, salt, and freshly ground pepper. It may be flavored with croutons of bread rubbed with fresh garlic or with dry or prepared Dijon-style mustard. Fresh tarragon, chives, savory, chervil, or parsley may be snipped into the salad, or these same herbs, dried, may be rubbed between the palms of the hands to release the flavor and then mixed with the dressing.

The greens are carefully washed in cold water and dried, and then the salad is dressed just before serving. It is eaten without accompaniment and is expected to refresh the palate.

Green Salad

SALADE VERTE

1 small head Boston lettuce	½ small head romaine
1 small head Bibb lettuce	1 Belgian endive

½ clove garlic
6 tablespoons olive oil
3 tablespoons tarragon vinegar

1 teaspoon salt
Freshly ground black pepper

1. Prepare salad greens: Wash lettuce, romaine, and endive, and separate into leaves, discarding discolored or bruised leaves. Drain well, shaking in salad basket or placing on paper towels, to remove excess moisture.

2. Place cleaned greens in plastic bag, or wrap in plastic film. Refrigerate until crisp and cold—several hours. Also refrigerate salad bowl.

3. At serving time, rub inside of salad bowl with garlic; discard garlic. Tear greens in bite-size pieces into bowl; leave small leaves whole.

4. In jar with tight-fitting lid, combine oil, vinegar, salt, and dash pepper; shake until well combined.

5. Pour half of dressing over greens. With salad spoon and fork, toss greens until they are well coated and no dressing remains in bottom of bowl. Add more dressing, if desired.

Makes 6 to 8 servings.

Green Salad with Fresh Herb Dressing

SALADE VERTE AUX FINES HERBES

Fresh Herb Dressing
½ cup salad oil
¼ cup tarragon vinegar
1 tablespoon snipped chives
1 tablespoon snipped fresh dill,
  or 1 teaspoon dried dill weed
½ clove garlic, crushed
1 teaspoon sugar
1 teaspoon salt

Dash pepper

1 small head Boston lettuce,
  washed and chilled
2 Belgian endives, washed
  and chilled
2 tablespoons chopped parsley
6 sprigs watercress

1. Make Fresh Herb Dressing: In jar with tight-fitting lid, combine oil, vinegar, chives, dill, garlic, sugar, salt, and pepper; shake well. Refrigerate until well chilled—at least 1 hour.

2. Tear the lettuce and endives in bite-size pieces into salad bowl. Add parsley.

3. Shake dressing vigorously; pour over salad. Toss until greens are well coated. Garnish with watercress.

Makes 6 to 8 servings.

Chicory and Watercress Salad Bowl

SALADE D'ENDIVE ET CRESSON

1 medium head chicory	⅛ teaspoon pepper
1 small bunch watercress	⅛ teaspoon sugar
¾ cup salad oil	1 clove garlic, slivered
¼ cup vinegar	2 hard-cooked eggs
¼ teaspoon salt	

1. Wash chicory and watercress in cold water; dry on paper towels. Tear into bite-size pieces.

2. Toss chicory and watercress in a large bowl. Then refrigerate, covered, for 1 hour.

3. Meanwhile, in jar with tight-fitting lid, combine oil, vinegar, salt, pepper, sugar, and garlic; shake to combine well. Refrigerate.

4. Press egg yolks and whites separately through sieve; set aside.

5. Just before using dressing, remove and discard garlic. Add egg white; shake well. Toss lightly with salad greens.

6. Sprinkle egg yolk around edge of salad bowl, to form a border. Serve at once.

Makes 8 servings.

Endive and Romaine Salad

SALADE DE CHICORÉE ET ROMAINE

1 large head romaine	½ teaspoon dried tarragon
3 Belgian endives	leaves
2 pint boxes cherry	1 bottle (8 ounces) herb-and-
tomatoes	garlic French dressing

1. Wash romaine and endives; separate into leaves. Halve lengthwise large outer leaves of romaine. Wash tomatoes and destem.

2. Add tarragon to salad dressing.

3. Mound tomatoes in center of salad bowl; line side of bowl first with romaine leaves, then with endive leaves. Pour dressing over greens.

Makes 8 to 10 servings.

Desserts

French desserts are both elaborate and rich or simple and unpretentious, depending on whether they are to be the ending of an elegant dinner or a family supper. The dessert is as carefully decided upon as the rest of the meal. A rich chocolate cake never follows a hearty dinner of Boeuf Bourguignon. Instead, a light soufflé, custard, or fruit tart is served. A light meal of fish or chicken allows the diner to appreciate properly desserts like Crêpes Suzette or Pots de Crème.

French desserts vary in elaborateness and length of preparation time. Desserts based on puff-pastry or decorated cakes take hours to prepare, and a perfect result usually requires a certain amount of experience on the cook's part. However, an impressive soufflé can be whipped together in about 20 minutes. An authentic French dessert, therefore, need not be time-consuming, and many desserts like fruit tarts, custards, and chilled mousses can be prepared the day before they are needed.

Hot desserts are usually served in the colder months. Soufflés, crêpes, or the warm apple tarts typical of Normandy are not considered suitable for the summer when the French like lighter meals. Warm weather desserts are tarts made with fruits as they come into season, mousses or chilled and molded soufflés, Bavarian creams flavored with fresh fruit, and molded custards.

Many of the desserts in this chapter are not served daily in French households, but are reserved for the main Sunday meal, family celebrations, or formal dinners. The everyday dessert is fresh fruit, often eaten with cheese. Fruit may be eaten individually or cut up and combined in a macédoine, flavored with a liqueur. The fruit of France is magnificent, perfumed and flavorful. One of the earliest of the seasonal fruits is the wild strawberry, fraises de bois; then peaches, apricots, plums; Montmorency cherries from near Paris, pears, and apples from Normandy follow.

The French dessert cheeses are deservedly famous, and most of them perfectly complement fresh fruit. The delicate double- and triple-crème cheeses (Gourmandise, Triple-Crème Parfait, and Boursault) should be accompanied by berries, peaches, currants, or strawberry or quince jam. They are served with fresh bread, as are all the French cheeses eaten after the main course. Coeur à la Crème, made from cream cheese and eaten with strawberries or raspberries, can substitute for these soft, delicately flavored cheeses when they are not available.

Other cheeses to be enjoyed with fruit are Brie and Camembert, both excellent with apples, pears, and grapes; Coulommier with peaches, apricots, and pineapple; Pont l'Éveque and the stronger Cantal with tart apples, pears, and green grapes; and the masterful Roquefort with tart apples and pears.

Raspberries Sabayon

SABAYON AUX FRAMBOISES

Sabayon Sauce:
4 egg yolks
2 tablespoons sugar
¼ cup Grand Marnier
⅓ cup heavy cream, whipped

2 pint boxes red raspberries, washed and drained; or 3 packages (10-ounce size) frozen raspberries, thawed and drained

1. Make Sabayon Sauce: In top of double boiler, with electric mixer at medium speed, beat egg yolks until thick. Gradually beat in sugar; beat until mixture is light and soft peaks form when beater is slowly raised.

2. Place double-boiler top over simmering water (water in bottom should not touch base of top). Slowly beat in Grand Marnier; continue beating until mixture is fluffy and mounds—takes about 5 minutes.

3. Remove double-boiler top from hot water; set in ice water. Beat the custard mixture until cool. Gently fold in whipped cream.

4. Refrigerate sauce, covered, until serving.

5. Place berries in serving bowl or dessert dishes. Stir sauce; pour over fruit.

Makes 6 servings.

Caramel Custard

CRÈME CARAMEL

1½ cups sugar	⅛ teaspoon salt
1 quart milk	1 teaspoon vanilla extract
6 eggs	

1. Preheat oven to 325°F. Place 1 cup sugar in a heavy skillet; cook over low heat, without stirring, until the sugar forms a light brown syrup. Then stir to blend.

2. Use to coat 1½-quart casserole. Hold dish with pot holder, and slowly pour in hot syrup, turning to coat bottom and side.

3. Make custard: In medium saucepan over medium heat, heat the milk just until bubbles form around edge of the saucepan.

4. In large bowl, with rotary beater, beat eggs slightly. Add remaining ½ cup sugar, the salt, and vanilla. Gradually pour in hot milk, stirring constantly. Pour into casserole.

5. Set casserole in shallow pan; pour hot water to ½-inch level around dish.

6. Bake 1 hour and 35 minutes, or until silver knife inserted in center comes out clean. Let custard cool; then refrigerate overnight.

7. To serve: Run small spatula around edge of casserole, to loosen. Invert on shallow serving dish; shake gently to release. The caramel acts as a sauce.

Makes 8 servings.

Creole Baked Custard

CRÈME BRÛLÉE

This is actually a Creole dessert, a variation on the classic French crème anglaise by Louisiana chefs.

3 cups heavy cream	1 teaspoon vanilla extract
6 egg yolks	⅓ cup light brown sugar,
⅓ cup granulated sugar	packed

1. Heat cream in heavy saucepan just until bubbles form around the edge of the pan.

2. In double-boiler top, with electric mixer, beat yolks with granulated sugar until thick and light yellow. Gradually stir in cream.

3. Place over hot, not boiling water; cook, stirring constantly, until it coats a metal spoon—about 15 minutes. Add the vanilla.

4. Strain custard into a 1-quart, shallow baking dish. Refrigerate 8 hours or overnight.

5. Just before serving, carefully sift brown sugar evenly over surface. Set dish in baking pan; surround with ice. Run under broiler just until sugar melts slightly and caramelizes—it will form a crust.

Makes 8 servings.

Vanilla Cup Custard

POTS DE CRÈME À LA VANILLE

3 cups heavy cream	5 egg yolks
½ cup sugar	
1 tablespoon vanilla extract	Chocolate Curls, page 110

1. Preheat oven to 325°F. Place 8 (5-ounce) custard cups or 10 (3-ounce) pot-de-crème cups in a baking pan.

2. In medium saucepan, combine cream and sugar; cook over medium heat, stirring occasionally, until sugar is dissolved and mixture is hot. Remove from heat; stir in vanilla.

3. In medium bowl, with wire whisk or rotary beater, beat egg yolks until blended—not frothy. Gradually add cream mixture, stirring constantly.

4. Strain, using fine strainer, into 4-cup measure. (If desired, first line strainer with cheesecloth.) Pour into cups.

5. Set baking pan on oven rack. Pour hot water to ½-inch level around cups.

6. Bake 25 to 30 minutes, or until mixture just begins to set around edges.

7. Immediately remove cups from water, and place on wire rack. Let cool 30 minutes; then refrigerate, each covered with plastic film, foil, or lid, till chilled—at least 4 hours.

8. To serve: Top with sweetened whipped cream, if desired. Then garnish with chocolate curls.

Makes 8 or 10 servings.

Chocolate Mousse

MOUSSE AU CHOCOLAT

5 egg whites, at room temperature	2 teaspoons lemon juice
¼ teaspoon cream of tartar	4 squares unsweetened chocolate, melted and cooled
1 cup sugar	1⅔ cups heavy cream
5 egg yolks	
⅛ teaspoon salt	Chocolate Curls, page 110

1. In large bowl, with electric mixer at high speed, beat egg whites with cream of tartar until soft peaks form when beater is slowly raised. Gradually add ¾ cup sugar, 2 tablespoons at a time, beating well after each addition; continue to beat until stiff peaks form.

2. In small bowl, with same beater, beat egg yolks with salt until thick and lemon-colored. Gradually add remaining sugar, beating well after each addition.

3. Gradually beat in lemon juice, melted chocolate, and ⅓ cup cream until mixture is smooth and thickened.

4. Beat remaining cream until stiff. Fold with chocolate mixture into egg whites. Gently turn into a 2-quart serving dish, spreading evenly.

5. Refrigerate 24 hours.

6. To serve: Decorate top of mousse with additional whipped cream and semisweet-chocolate curls, if desired.

Makes 8 servings.

Lemon Soufflé in Lemon Shells

SOUFFLÉ AU CITRON

2 eggs	⅛ teaspoon salt
6 extra large lemons	¼ cup milk
2 ladyfingers	1 tablespoon grated lemon peel
1½ teaspoons Cointreau	1 tablespoon butter or regular margarine
2 tablespoons flour	⅛ teaspoon cream of tartar
5 tablespoons sugar	

1. Separate eggs, putting whites in medium bowl and yolks in small bowl. Let whites warm to room temperature—about 1 hour.

2. Meanwhile, cut 1 inch from blossom end of each lemon. With grapefruit knife, remove fruit, holding over bowl to catch juice and being careful not to cut through peel. Measure 2 tablespoons juice; set

aside. Scrape out inside to make smooth shells. With paring knife or scissors, scallop edge if you wish. Cut a sliver of peel off bottom if shells do not stand evenly. Place shells in small baking pan.

3. Separate halves of ladyfingers. Cut each in half crosswise. Place a piece in each lemon shell, and sprinkle ¼ teaspoon Cointreau over each ladyfinger piece.

4. In small, heavy saucepan, mix flour, sugar, and salt. Slowly stir in ¼ cup water and the milk, stirring until smooth. Cook over medium heat, stirring constantly, until mixture is thickened and begins to boil. Remove from heat.

5. With wire whisk or fork, beat egg yolks. Stir half of hot sauce mixture into egg yolks; return mixture to saucepan, stirring. Cook over medium heat, stirring constantly, until mixture just begins to bubble. Remove from heat.

6. Add reserved lemon juice, the grated peel, and butter; beat until well blended. Cool about 10 minutes.

7. Meanwhile, preheat oven to 375°F.

8. Add cream of tartar to egg whites. With electric beater at high speed, beat until stiff peaks form when beater is slowly raised.

9. Fold half of egg whites into lemon mixture until well combined. Carefully fold in remaining whites just until combined.

10. Spoon soufflé mixture into prepared lemon shells, filling to rim. Bake 30 minutes, or until well puffed and lightly browned on top. Sprinkle tops with confectioners' sugar if you wish. Serve at once.

Makes 6 servings.

Molded Cream Cheese Heart

COEUR À LA CRÈME

The French would eat this delectable cheese with fresh bread, but it is equally good with unsalted crackers. Raspberries can be substituted for the strawberries.

2 packages (8-ounce size) soft cream cheese	2 tablespoons confectioners' sugar
¼ cup heavy cream	1 pint box fresh strawberries

1. Line a 7-inch heart-shaped basket with cheesecloth.

2. In medium bowl, with portable electric mixer at medium speed, beat cream cheese until light and fluffy.

3. Gradually add cream, beating until smooth and well combined. Beat in sugar.

4. Pack cream-cheese mixture firmly into basket; cover with waxed paper or Saran. Refrigerate overnight.

5. Next day, wash and drain strawberries; do not hull. Refrigerate until ready to use.

6. To serve: Unmold Coeur à la Crème onto serving plate. Surround with whole strawberries.

Makes 6 servings.

Upside-down Apple Tart

TARTE TATIN

1 cup sugar	½ package (9½-ounce size)
½ cup butter or margarine	piecrust mix
8 medium apples	Whipped cream
(about 3½ pounds)	

1. Place sugar in 10-inch heavy skillet with heat-resistant handle. Cook over medium heat until it melts and becomes a light brown syrup. Remove from heat; add butter, stirring until melted.

2. Pare, quarter, and core apples. Arrange in a layer, rounded side down, in sugar mixture. Make a second layer, rounded side up, fitting the pieces between pieces in first layer. If open spaces remain, fill with slices of apple.

3. Preheat oven to 450°F.

4. Prepare piecrust mix as package label directs for one-crust pie. On lightly floured surface, roll pastry to a 10-inch circle. Place over apples.

5. Bake 25 to 30 minutes, or until crust is golden brown. Invert onto shallow serving dish. Serve lukewarm. Garnish with whipped cream and, if desired, crystallized violets.

Makes 6 to 8 servings.

Fresh Strawberry Tart

TARTE AUX FRAISES

Tart Shell	2 tablespoons granulated
¼ cup butter or regular	sugar
margarine, softened	3 tablespoons almond paste

½ teaspoon grated lemon peel
1 egg white
¾ cup sifted all-purpose flour

Rum Cream
1 teaspoon unflavored
    gelatine
2 tablespoons granulated
    sugar
2 tablespoons flour
Salt
1 egg yolk

½ cup milk
2 tablespoons rum
1 egg white, stiffly beaten
½ cup heavy cream
1 tablespoon confectioners' sugar
1 inch vanilla bean, scraped

1½ pint boxes strawberries,
    washed and hulled
½ recipe Currant-Jelly Glaze,
    page 108

1. Make Tart Shell: Grease and lightly flour an 8-by-1½-inch round layer-cake pan.

2. In a medium bowl, with electric mixer at medium speed, cream butter with 2 tablespoons granulated sugar, the almond paste, and lemon peel until well combined.

3. Add 1 egg white; beat at high speed until smooth. Gradually beat in ¾ cup flour until well blended. Turn into prepared pan; pat evenly over bottom and side. (If too soft to work with, refrigerate 10 minutes.) Refrigerate 1 hour or longer.

4. Preheat oven to 300°F. Bake shell 50 minutes, or until golden brown. Let cool in pan on wire rack 15 minutes; then gently turn out onto rack, and let cool completely.

5. Make Rum Cream: In small saucepan, mix gelatine, granulated sugar, flour, and dash salt; mix well.

6. Beat egg yolk with milk and rum. Add to gelatine mixture; cook over medium heat, stirring constantly with wire whisk, until mixture is thickened and comes to boiling.

7. Pour into medium bowl; set bowl in pan of ice and water; let stand, stirring occasionally, until mixture begins to set—about 8 to 10 minutes. Fold in beaten egg white.

8. Beat cream with confectioners' sugar; fold into gelatine mixture. Stir in scraped vanilla bean. Spread evenly over tart shell. Refrigerate 30 minutes.

9. Arrange berries on rum cream in shell; brush with Currant-Jelly Glaze. Refrigerate until serving.

Makes 8 servings.

Fruit Tartlets

TARTELETTES AUX FRUITS REFRAÎCHIS

Tart Shells
½ cup butter or regular
   margarine, softened
¼ cup sugar
¼ teaspoon salt
1 egg white
1½ cups sifted all-purpose
   flour

Praline Paste, page 110
Rum Cream, see
   Strawberry Tart, page 95

Fruits: whole strawberries,
   blueberries, red raspberries,
   sliced bananas, seedless green
   grapes, apricot halves, black
   cherries (fresh, frozen, or
   canned), canned small pineapple rings or tidbits

Apricot Glaze or Currant-Jelly
   Glaze, page 108

1. Make Tart Shells: In medium bowl, with fork, blend butter, sugar, salt, and egg white until smooth and well combined.

2. Gradually stir in flour, mixing until smooth.

3. For each tart, use 2 teaspoons dough. Press evenly into assorted 2½- to 3-inch tart pans. Set pans on cookie sheet.

4. Refrigerate 30 minutes.

5. Preheat oven to 375°F. Bake tart shells 12 to 15 minutes, or until light golden. Cool in pans on wire rack a few minutes; then turn out, and cool completely before filling.

6. To fill tarts: Spoon about 1¼ teaspoons Praline Paste into each shell, then 1 to 2 teaspoons Rum Cream. Refrigerate.

7. Top with fruit. (Drain fruit very well before using.) Brush yellow or light fruit with warm Apricot Glaze and red or dark fruit with Currant-Jelly Glaze.

8. Refrigerate until ready to serve.

Makes 1½ dozen.

Note: If desired, make Tart Shells, Praline Paste, and Rum Cream day before. Then assemble tarts several hours before serving.

Crêpes Flamed with Orange Butter

CRÊPES SUZETTE

This is a dessert that is ideal for entertaining because the crêpes can be made ahead of time and then the dessert can be finished in a chafing dish at the table. Make the crêpes in the morning, place them between squares of waxed paper, and store in the refrigerator. The Orange Butter and Orange Sauce may be made at the same time. At serving time, follow the instructions in paragraph 7, heating the crêpes and sauce in the chafing dish pan on the kitchen stove before bringing it to the table (see paragraph 8).

Crêpes
1 cup unsifted all-purpose
    flour
¼ cup butter or margarine,
    melted and cooled; or
    ¼ cup salad oil
2 eggs
2 egg yolks
1½ cups milk

Orange Butter
¾ cup sweet butter
½ cup sugar
⅓ cup Grand Marnier

¼ cup grated orange peel

Orange Sauce
½ cup sweet butter
¾ cup sugar
2 tablespoons shredded orange
    peel
⅔ cup orange juice
2 oranges, peeled and
    sectioned
½ cup Grand Marnier

Butter or margarine
3 tablespoons Grand Marnier

1. Make Crêpes: In medium bowl, combine flour, melted butter, eggs, egg yolks, and ½ cup milk; beat with rotary beater until smooth. Beat in the remaining milk until mixture is well blended.

2. Refrigerate, covered, at least 2 hours.

3. Meanwhile, make Orange Butter: In small bowl, with electric mixer, cream ¾ cup sweet butter with ½ cup sugar until light and fluffy. Add ⅓ cup Grand Marnier and ¼ cup orange peel; beat until well blended. Set aside.

4. Make Orange Sauce: In large skillet, melt sweet butter. Stir in sugar, orange peel, and orange juice; cook over low heat, stirring occasionally, until peel is translucent—about 20 minutes. Add orange sections and ½ cup Grand Marnier. Keep warm.

5. To cook crêpes: Slowly heat an 8-inch skillet until a drop of water sizzles and rolls off. For each crêpe, brush skillet lightly with butter. Pour in about 2 tablespoons batter, rotating pan quickly, to spread batter completely over bottom of skillet.

6. Cook until lightly browned; then turn, and brown other side. Turn out onto wire rack.

7. Spread each crêpe with Orange Butter, dividing evenly. Fold

each in half, then in half again. When all are folded, place in Orange Sauce in chafing dish or skillet; cook over low heat until heated through.

8. To serve: Gently heat 3 tablespoons Grand Marnier in small saucepan just until vapor rises. Ignite with match, and pour over crêpes. Serve flaming.

Makes 6 to 8 servings.

Rum Baba

BABA AU RHUM

Babas and Savarins are both sweet yeast breads, flavored with rum syrup. They are impressive desserts without being overly rich. They seem most suitable to serve when only a dessert and coffee are necessary, such as after a bridge game or an afternoon committee meeting.

¾ cup warm water
    (105° to 115°F)
2 packages active dry yeast
¼ cup sugar
1 teaspoon salt
6 eggs
3¾ cups sifted all-purpose
    flour
¾ cup soft butter or
    margarine
½ cup finely chopped citron
¼ cup currants or
    seedless raisins

Rum Syrup
2½ cups sugar
2 cups water
1 medium unpeeled orange,
    sliced crosswise
½ unpeeled lemon, sliced
    crosswise
1 to 1½ cups light rum

Apricot Glaze
1 cup apricot preserves
1 teaspoon grated lemon peel
2 teaspoons lemon juice

1. Lightly grease a 10-by-4-inch tube pan. If possible, check temperature of warm water with thermometer.

2. Sprinkle yeast over water in large bowl of electric mixer; stir until dissolved.

3. Add ¼ cup sugar, the salt, eggs, and 2¼ cups flour. At medium speed, beat 4 minutes, or until smooth, scraping side of bowl and guiding mixture into beater with rubber scraper.

4. Add butter; beat 2 minutes, or until very well blended.

5. At low speed, beat in rest of flour; beat until smooth—about 2 minutes.

6. Stir in citron and currants. Batter will be thick.

7. Turn batter into prepared pan, spreading evenly. Cover with towel.

8. Let rise in warm place (85°F), free from drafts, 1 hour and 10 minutes, or until baba has risen to within ½ inch of top of pan.

9. Meanwhile, preheat oven to 400°F. Gently place baba on oven rack (do not jar; baba might fall).

10. Bake 40 to 45 minutes, or until it is deep golden brown and cake tester inserted in center comes out clean.

11. Meanwhile, make Rum Syrup: In medium saucepan, combine sugar with 2 cups water; bring to boiling, stirring until sugar is dissolved. Boil, uncovered, 10 minutes.

12. Reduce heat. Add orange and lemon slices; simmer 10 minutes. Remove from heat. Add rum.

13. With metal spatula, carefully loosen sides of baba from pan. Turn out of pan onto wire rack; let cool 15 minutes. Return baba to pan.

14. Set pan on large sheet of foil. Gradually pour hot syrup, along with fruit slices, over baba. Continue pouring until all syrup is absorbed.

15. Let baba stand 2 hours or longer.

16. Meanwhile, make Apricot Glaze: In small saucepan, over low heat, melt apricot preserves. Stir in lemon peel and juice; strain. Refrigerate 30 minutes or until ready to use.

17. To serve baba: Discard fruit slices. Turn out baba into round serving platter. Brush top and side with apricot glaze.

18. If desired, serve with whipped cream.

Makes 12 to 16 servings.

Savarin with Fresh Fruit

SAVARIN

Savarin
¼ cup warm water
  (105° to 115°F)
1 package active dry yeast
2 tablespoons sugar
¼ teaspoon salt
2 eggs
¼ cup butter or regular
  margarine, softened
1¾ cups sifted all-purpose
  flour

Rum Syrup
1¼ cups sugar
3 slices lemon

3 slices orange
¾ cup golden rum

Apricot Glaze
1 cup apricot preserves
1 tablespoon lemon juice

2 medium pears
2 navel oranges
1 pint box strawberries
2 cups seedless green grapes
Sweetened whipped cream

1. Make Savarin: If possible, check temperature of water with thermometer. Sprinkle yeast over water in medium bowl; stir until dissolved. Add 2 tablespoons sugar, the salt, eggs, butter, and 1 cup flour. Using wooden spoon, mix until well blended; then beat until batter is smooth and leaves sides of bowl—2 to 3 minutes. Add remaining flour; beat until smooth.

2. Cover with towel; let rise in warm place (85°F), free from drafts, until double in bulk—about 1 hour.

3. Generously grease a 5-cup ring mold. Spoon batter evenly into prepared mold. Cover with towel; let rise to top of pan—about 45 minutes.

4. Preheat oven to 375°F. Bake savarin 20 to 25 minutes, or until nicely browned.

5. Meanwhile, make Rum Syrup: In medium saucepan, combine sugar with 1½ cups water; bring to boiling, stirring, until sugar is dissolved. Boil, uncovered, 10 minutes. Reduce heat; add lemon and orange slices; simmer 10 minutes. Remove from heat; add rum.

6. Remove savarin to wire rack; let cool 10 minutes. Loosen around edge with spatula; turn into 9-inch layer-cake pan. With cake tester, punch holes in savarin at 1-inch intervals.

7. Remove fruit slices from rum syrup; set aside ½ cup syrup. Spoon half of remaining syrup over savarin; let stand, 30 minutes. Spoon other half of syrup over savarin; let stand 30 minutes.

8. Meanwhile, make Apricot Glaze: In small saucepan, combine preserves and lemon juice; heat, stirring, until melted. Strain.

9. Carefully remove savarin to serving plate. Spread glaze over savarin. Refrigerate until serving time.

10. Prepare fruit: Pare, core, and cut pears in eighths. Peel oranges, and section. Wash, hull, and slice strawberries. Wash grapes. Place fruit in large bowl; add reserved rum syrup. Refrigerate, covered, until serving time.

11. To serve: Remove fruit from bowl with slotted spoon, and mound in center of savarin. If desired, decorate with orange slices, whole strawberries, and grapes. Serve with bowl of whipped cream.

Makes 8 to 10 servings.

Madeleines

2 eggs	1 cup sifted all-purpose
1 cup granulated sugar	flour

¾ cup butter or margarine, melted and cooled	1 teaspoon grated lemon peel Confectioners' sugar

1. Preheat oven to 350°F. Grease and lightly flour madeleine pans.

2. In top of double boiler, over hot, not boiling, water (water in bottom of double boiler should not touch base of pan above), with electric mixer at medium speed, beat eggs and granulated sugar while mixture heats to lukewarm—takes about 2 minutes.

3. Set top of double boiler in cold water. Beat egg mixture, at high speed, 5 minutes, or until very light and fluffy.

4. With wire whisk or rubber scraper, gently fold in flour until well combined. Stir in cooled butter and lemon peel just until blended. Pour into prepared pans, using 1 tablespoon batter for each pan.

5. Bake 12 to 15 minutes, or until golden. Cool 1 minute. Then remove from pans with a small spatula; cool completely on wire racks. Then sprinkle with confectioners' sugar.

Makes 3½ dozen.

Chocolate Meringues with Ice Cream

MERINGUES GLACÉES AU CHOCOLAT

Chocolate Meringues	¼ teaspoon vanilla extract
1 egg white	1½ pints vanilla ice cream
½ cup sugar	
2 tablespoons grated unsweetened chocolate	Chocolate Sauce, page 109

1. Preheat oven to 300°F. Grease a cookie sheet.

2. Make Chocolate Meringues: In small bowl, with electric mixer at high speed, beat egg white just until soft peaks form when beater is slowly raised.

3. Add sugar, 1 tablespoon at a time, beating well after each addition. Continue beating until stiff peaks form when batter is slowly raised.

4. Fold in chocolate and vanilla just until blended. Drop by heaping tablespoonfuls, 1 inch apart, onto prepared cookie sheet, to make 12 mounds.

5. Bake 15 minutes. Turn off oven heat; leave meringues in oven 1½ to 2 hours, or until completely dry and crisp.

6. To serve: For each serving, place a ball of ice cream in a dessert

dish. Press a meringue, rounded side out, against one side, another against opposite side. Pass Chocolate Sauce.

Makes 6 servings.

Chocolate Cake

GÁTEAU AU CHOCOLAT

This cake is so rich that it is not iced but simply decorated with chocolate curls. The texture is moist and heavy, almost like a pudding. It keeps well under refrigeration.

4 eggs	4 teaspoons sugar
4 bars (4-ounce size) German's sweet cooking chocolate	4 teaspoons all-purpose flour
½ cup soft sweet butter	Chocolate Curls, page 110

1. Lightly grease a 9-by-5-by-3-inch loaf pan; line with waxed paper. Separate eggs, placing whites and yolks in large bowls. Let whites warm to room temperature—about 1 hour.

2. Preheat oven to 425°F.

3. In top of double boiler, melt chocolate over hot, not boiling, water, stirring occasionally. Remove from water; beat in butter with spoon.

4. Meanwhile, with portable electric mixer, beat egg whites until stiff peaks form when beater is slowly raised. Set aside.

5. With same beater, beat yolks until thick and lemon-colored. Slowly add sugar, beating constantly. Add flour; beat just until blended.

6. Stir into chocolate mixture. Then, with rubber scraper or a wire whisk, gently fold chocolate mixture into beaten egg white.

7. Turn into prepared pan. Reduce over temperature to 350°F. Bake 25 minutes.

8. Let cool completely in pan on wire rack. Cake will settle like a cheesecake. Refrigerate until well chilled—about 4 hours.

9. To serve: Loosen cake; remove from pan by inverting on serving plate. If desired, decorate with chocolate curls. Cut cake into ¾-inch slices.

Makes 16 servings.

Cream-Puff Dough

PÂTE À CHOU

Light-as-air cream puffs and éclairs are the result with this basic recipe. Both should not be filled and frosted until shortly before serving.

½ cup water
¼ cup butter or regular
   margarine
⅛ teaspoon salt

½ cup unsifted all-purpose
   flour
2 eggs

1. In small saucepan, combine ½ cup water, the butter, and salt. Bring to boiling over medium heat.

2. Remove from heat. Immediately, with wooden spoon, beat in flour all at once.

3. Return to low heat, and continue beating until mixture forms a ball and leaves sides of pan.

4. Remove from heat. Add eggs, one at a time, beating hard after each addition until smooth. Continue beating until the mixture is shiny and breaks in strands.

Note: To make double recipe of Cream-Puff Dough: Make as above in medium saucepan, using 1 cup water, ½ cup butter or margarine, ¼ teaspoon salt, 1 cup flour, and 4 eggs.

Cream Puffs

CHOUX À LA CRÈME

Cream-Puff Dough, above
Whipped Cream Filling, page 106
   or
Coffee Chantilly Filling,
   page 107

Caramel Glaze, page 108

1. Make Cream-Puff Dough. Preheat oven to 400°F.

2. Drop dough by rounded tablespoonfuls, about 2 inches apart, onto ungreased cookie sheet, making 6 puffs.

3. Bake 45 minutes until puffed and golden brown. Puffs should sound hollow when lightly tapped with fingertip. Let cool completely on wire rack, away from any drafts.

4. With sharp knife, cut off tops crosswise. Scoop out any filaments of soft dough.

5. Fill with Whipped Cream Filling or Coffee Chantilly Filling. Replace tops. Frost with Caramel Glaze or sprinkle tops with confectioners' sugar.

Makes 6.

Ice Cream Filled Cream Puffs

PROFITEROLES

Cream-Puff Dough, page 104	½ cup heavy cream, whipped
2 pints strawberry ice cream	Chopped pistachios
Chocolate Sauce, page 109	

1. Preheat oven to 400°F. Make Cream-Puff Dough.

2. Drop dough by rounded half teaspoonfuls, 1 inch apart, onto ungreased cookie sheet, to make 40 puffs.

3. Bake 20 to 25 minutes, or until puffed and golden brown. Remove to wire rack; let cool completely.

4. Meanwhile, with large end of a melon-ball cutter or a 1-teaspoon measuring spoon, scoop ice cream into 40 balls. Place immediately in a chilled pan, and store in freezer.

5. Make Chocolate Sauce.

6. To assemble profiteroles: With sharp knife, cut a slice from top of each puff. Fill each with an ice-cream ball; replace top. (Place in freezer if not serving at once.)

7. To serve: Mound puffs in serving dish. Spoon chocolate sauce over top. Garnish with whipped cream and pistachios. For individual servings: In each dessert dish, mound 5 puffs. Spoon sauce over top. Garnish with whipped cream and pistachios.

Makes 8 servings.

FILLINGS, SAUCES, AND GLAZES

Chocolate Cream

¼ cup sugar	1 egg
1 tablespoon cornstarch	1 tablespoon butter or
Dash salt	margarine
1 cup milk	½ teaspoon vanilla
1 package (6 ounces) semisweet	extract
chocolate pieces (1 cup)	

1. In small saucepan, combine sugar, cornstarch, and salt. Gradually stir in milk; add chocolate.

2. Cook over medium heat, stirring constantly, until mixture boils; boil 1 minute. Remove from heat.

3. Lightly beat egg in small bowl. Gradually stir in a little hot mixture; then stir into rest of mixture in saucepan. Cook, stirring, until thick —about 2 minutes. Remove from heat; stir in butter and vanilla.

4. Cool to room temperature. Turn into bowl; refrigerate, covered. Makes 1¾ cups.

Almond Cream

1 envelope unflavored gelatine	6 egg yolks
4 cups milk	2 teaspoons vanilla extract
1 cup sugar	1 teaspoon almond extract
½ cup cornstarch	1 cup heavy cream
Dash salt	

1. Sprinkle gelatine over ¼ cup milk; let soften.

2. Meanwhile, in medium saucepan, heat remaining milk until tiny bubbles appear around the edge of the pan.

3. In small bowl, combine sugar, cornstarch, and salt; mix well. Gradually stir into hot milk. Cook over medium heat, stirring, until mixture boils and is thickened.

4. Stir in gelatine; boil 1 minute.

5. In small bowl, beat egg yolks slightly. Gradually add a little hot mixture, stirring constantly. Add to hot mixture in saucepan; cook, stirring, until mixture boils. Remove from heat.

6. Stir in extracts; pour into large bowl. Place sheet of waxed paper directly on surface of filling. Refrigerate until chilled—2 to 3 hours.

7. Whip cream until stiff. Add to chilled mixture; beat with rotary beater just until smooth. Refrigerate 1 hour longer, or until ready to use. Makes 5¾ cups.

Whipped Cream Filling

1 cup heavy cream	1 teaspoon vanilla extract
½ cup sifted confectioners' sugar	¼ teaspoon almond extract

1. In medium bowl, combine cream, sugar, and extracts.

2. Refrigerate, covered, at least 1 hour—until very well chilled. Refrigerate rotary beater also.

3. Beat mixture, with rotary beater, just until stiff.

Makes 2 cups; filling for 6 large puffs or éclairs.

Custard Filling

1½ cups milk	2 egg yolks
¼ cup sugar	1 teaspoon vanilla extract
1½ tablespoons cornstarch	

1. In small, heavy saucepan, slowly heat milk just until bubbles form around edge of pan.

2. Meanwhile, in small bowl, combine sugar and cornstarch; stir to mix well. Stir into hot milk, all at once.

3. Cook, stirring, over medium heat, until mixture boils. Reduce heat, and simmer 1 minute.

4. Beat a small amount of hot mixture into egg yolks. Pour back into saucepan; cook, stirring, over medium heat, until mixture boils and thickens. Stir in vanilla.

5. Place waxed paper directly on surface, to prevent film from forming. Refrigerate filling until ready to use.

Makes 1⅓ cups; filling for 6 puffs or éclairs.

Coffee Chantilly Filling

1 cup heavy cream	2 teaspoons instant coffee
½ cup sifted confectioners' sugar	1 teaspoon vanilla extract

1. In medium bowl, combine cream, sugar, coffee, and vanilla; mix well.

2. Refrigerate, covered, at least 1 hour—until very well chilled. Refrigerate rotary beater also.

3. Beat, with rotary beater, just until stiff.

Makes 2 cups; filling for 6 puffs or éclairs.

Chocolate Glaze

1 package (6 ounces) semi-sweet chocolate pieces	2 tablespoons light corn syrup
2 tablespoons shortening	3 tablespoons milk

1. In top of double boiler, over hot, not boiling, water, melt chocolate pieces with shortening.

2. Add corn syrup and milk, stirring until smooth and well blended. Let cool slightly.

3. Pour warm glaze over cooled, filled cream puffs placed on wire rack, with pan underneath.

Makes 1 cup.

Caramel Glaze

½ pound caramels   ½ cup water

1. Remove paper wrapping from caramels. Place caramels in top of double boiler with ¼ cup water.

2. Melt over hot, not boiling, water.

3. Stir to mix well. Pour warm glaze over cooled, filled cream puffs placed on a wire rack, with pan underneath.

Makes ¾ cup.

Apricot Glaze

½ cup apricot preserves

1. In small saucepan, over medium heat, stir apricot preserves until melted. (If preserves seem too thick, thin with ½ to 1 tablespoon hot water.)

2. Strain. Use warm, on tarts.

Makes about ½ cup.

Currant-Jelly Glaze

½ cup red-currant jelly   1 tablespoon kirsch

1. In small saucepan, over moderate heat, stir currant jelly until melted. Remove from heat.

2. Stir in kirsch. Use warm, on tarts. (If glaze becomes too thick, reheat gently, and add a little hot water.)

Makes about ½ cup.

Chocolate Sauce

¼ cup sugar
⅓ cup light cream
1 package (4 ounces) sweet
   cooking chocolate

1 square (1 ounce)
   unsweetened chocolate

1. In top of double boiler, combine sugar and 2 tablespoons cream; cook, over boiling water, until sugar is dissolved.

2. Cut up both kinds of chocolate. Remove double boiler from heat, but leave top over bottom. Add chocolate to cream mixture, stirring until melted.

3. With spoon, beat in remaining cream. Serve warm.

Makes about 1 cup.

Brandy Custard Sauce

1 package (3 ounces) vanilla-
   pudding and pie-filling mix
2½ cups milk

2 tablespoons brandy, or
1 teaspoon vanilla extract

1. Make vanilla pudding as package label directs, using 2½ cups milk. Stir in brandy or vanilla.

2. Turn into bowl; place waxed paper directly on surface. Refrigerate several hours. Stir before serving. Serve very cold.

Makes 2½ cups.

Strawberry Sauce

2 packages (10-ounce size)
   frozen strawberries, thawed

1 tablespoon cornstarch
½ cup currant jelly

1. Drain strawberries, reserving liquid. Add enough water to liquid to make 2 cups.

2. In small saucepan, blend liquid with cornstarch. Bring to boiling over medium heat, stirring constantly; boil 5 minutes. Stir in jelly until melted. Remove from heat. Add strawberries. Refrigerate, covered, until cold.

Makes about 3 cups.

Praline Paste

¼ cup sugar
½ cup coarsely chopped
pecans or hazelnuts

2 squares semisweet
chocolate, melted

1. Lightly butter an 8-by-11½-inch round layer-cake pan or small cookie sheet.

2. Melt sugar in small, heavy skillet, over low heat, shaking pan from side to side. Continue to cook, stirring, until syrup turns light golden. Remove from heat.

3. Add nuts, stirring until just coated with syrup. Quickly turn into prepared pan. (Mixture will harden almost immediately.)

4. When cool, break into 2-inch pieces. Blend in food blender, to grind pieces finely. Turn into small bowl; add chocolate, and mix well.

Makes ½ cup.

Chocolate Curls

1 1-ounce square semisweet
or unsweetened chocolate

1. Let chocolate square stand in paper wrapper in warm place about 15 minutes, just to soften slightly.

2. Unwrap chocolate and carefully draw vegetable parer across broad, flat surface of square for large curls. For smaller curls, draw parer across side of square.

Lift curls with a wooden pick, to avoid breaking.

Index